Abraham Joshua Heschel

Philosopher of Wonder

Abraham Joshua Heschel

Philosopher of Wonder

Our Thirty-Year Friendship and Dialogue

MAURICE S. FRIEDMAN

CASCADE *Books* · Eugene, Oregon

ABRAHAM JOSHUA HESCHEL—PHILOSOPHER OF WONDER
Our Thirty-Year Friendship and Dialogue

Cascade Books
An Imprint of Wipf and Stock Publishers
199 W. 8th Ave., Suite 3
Eugene, OR 97401

www.wipfandstock.com

ISBN 13: 978-1-62032-206-2

Cataloguing-in-Publication data:

Friedman, Maurice S.

Abraham Joshua Heschel—philosopher of wonder : our thirty-year friendship and dialogue / Maurice S. Friedman.

vi + 118 pp. ; 23 cm. Includes bibliographical references and index.

ISBN 13: 978-1-62032-206-2

1. Heschel, Abraham Joshua, 1907–1972. 2. Jewish philosophers. 3. Philosophy, Jewish. I. Title.

BM755 H34 F7 2012

Manufactured in the U.S.A.

Contents

Contents

Part One

Heschel the Person

1

Moral Grandeur and Spiritual Audacity

Meeting Heschel

In July 1945 I transferred from the Philadelphia Institute for the Feeble Minded (thirty miles from Philadelphia) to a Civilian Public Service Camp in Gatlinburg, Tennessee. It had been arranged that at Smokemont, North Carolina, a spike camp of Gatlinburg, a number of us conscientious objectors who had met at weekend retreats off and on during the past year and a half intended to establish a more permanent retreat where silent meditation and mystical devotion could be practiced more fully while we worked during the days. I was only the second member of our retreat to arrive, which was fatal for my mysticism because the first person to arrive tried to convert me to his high-church Anglicanism so I could join with him in taking life-vows by Easter at an Anglican monastery. He had no regard at all for my concern for silent meditation.

I have told this story at length in my memoir-novel *The Group Dance*.

Meanwhile I had changed my primary devotion and loyalty from the non-dualistic Vedanta of Ramakrishna and Vivekenanda to Hasidism. What is more, my participation in a number of amateur psychodramas in Chapel Hill, North Carolina, during furloughs and weekends off, had brought me to a state in which I was no longer capable of meditating, as I had been doing the past year and half, nor was I any longer able to live up to my own goal of celibacy. None of this meant, however, that I had turned entirely away from mysticism, which has remained a personal and academic interest of mine throughout my life, including books and courses in comparative mysticism. When I was doing my doctoral work at the University of Chicago, my great teacher Joachim Wach complained to my young friend Arthur A. Cohen (years later a famous author and editor, but only 19 years old at the time) that I wore my mysticism on my sleeve!

My stint at Chapel Hill ended with my defying the leader of our psychodrama group and marrying Susan Lindsay, daughter of the famous American poet Vachel Lindsay, and taking off for Philadelphia. While there, I took Susan to meet Rabbi Simon Greenberg with whom I had met a number of times while stationed at the Institute near Philadelphia. Rabbi Greenberg proposed that we should go to New York City to meet Abraham Joshua Heschel, sending along with us a very nice note saying that one rarely meets young people like Susan and me these days. Heschel, who had only a few years before been rescued from certain death in Poland when the Hebrew Union

College–Jewish Institute of Religion in Cincinnati brought him to teach there ("I was a brand plucked from the flame," he was later to write), was now a young Professor of Jewish Mysticism and Ethics at the Jewish Theological Seminary in New York City, the institution that trained conservative rabbis just as the Hebrew Union College in Cincinnati, from which Heschel had only just transferred, trained Reform Rabbis. At that time, Professor Heschel did not yet have a beard (I was sorry when he later grew one since it made him seem more distant to me).

When Susan and I came to see Dr. Heschel, he was warm and cordial. It was winter time, and he commented on how remarkable it was that one could turn on a radiator and get heat—an example of the abiding wonder that was the basis of his philosophy of religion.[1] Heschel called the wonder that overcame him in his meeting with everyday things and events "awareness of the ineffable." When I wrote an essay on Heschel for a Hebrew book to which I contributed a number of years later, I dubbed him "the philosopher of wonder," which is also the subtitle of this book.

Meanwhile my wife of two months left me for my Harvard roommate and friend John Conrad Russell, son of the great British mathematician and philosopher Bertrand Russell. When I came to see Heschel again, I was anything but happy. "The Hasidim live by joy," Heschel, who was

---

1. I cannot help thinking of the reviewer for *The New York Times Book Review* of my 1987 book *Abraham Joshua Heschel and Elie Wiesel: "You Are My Witnesses"* who heaped scorn on me for mentioning in my book that when Heschel and I walked from the Jewish Theological Seminary to his apartment on Riverside Drive, Heschel made a point of our stopping to get orange juice!

5

himself the direct descendant of a long line of Hasidic *zaddikim* (the leaders of the Hasidic community) reaching all the way back to Dov Baer, the great Maggid of Mezritch, who succeeded the Baal Shem Tov and organized and through his disciples spread Hasidism throughout Eastern Europe after the death of the Besht. "If you cannot find joy in six weeks, do not come and see me again!" Heschel said to me. Later Heschel explained to me that the joy of the Hasidim came precisely through suffering and not through the absence of suffering.

Still under the spell of the amateur psychodrama that Susan and I took part in at Chapel Hill, I made a disparaging remark to Heschel about my mother. Heschel, whose mother and sister had been murdered by the Nazis only a few years before, cried out, "If I could find my mother, to tie her shoe laces, I would be the happiest man on earth!"

Largely ignorant of Hasidism and still more American Hasidism, I wanted to give my life to reviving Hasidism in America. Even though my background in Hebrew and Judaism was pitifully thin, Heschel sensed the genuineness of my love for Hasidism and was ready to help me. What I really would have liked at that point was a Jewish yoga that gave directions in meditation and prayer. Heschel would not give it to me, holding that Hasidism was an integral part of Judaism. It was only many years later that I discovered that there was indeed a book that gave the instructions that I longed for (a book by Arye Cohen, I believe). By then, however, it was no longer a live option for me. So synchronicity also works in a negative fashion!

Heschel once stressed that I was better off, from his point of view, to have had a thin background in Judaism in Tulsa yet remained Jewish than Franz Rosenzweig's great friend Eugen Rosenstock-Huessy, who came of a Jewish background but converted to Christianity. I think he was right, yet I often felt that Heschel could not really understand that my total lack of practical background in Halakhah—the Jewish law—was more of an obstacle to my joining him in the practice of Jewish law than any choice against it based on principle!

Heschel wanted me to go to the Jewish Theological Seminary, saying that there would be time enough when I graduated for me to find my way forward as rabbi, writer, journalist, or what have you. Simon Greenberg offered me $500 from his Har Zion temple fund to study Hebrew. Dr. Heschel and Rabbi Greenberg told me not to worry about the fact that I could not yet make the affirmation of the Jewish law that is a prerequisite for entering the Jewish Theological Seminary. It would come of itself in due time. Maybe they were right; yet it seemed to me less than honest to assume that such belief would come when I had no trace of it now. I was also troubled at the time, as I would not have been later, by the exclusiveness that I felt would result from my going to the seminary and becoming a rabbi.

Martin Buber wrote that it had sometimes been suggested to him that he should liberate Hasidism from its confessional limitations and make of it a universal religion of mankind. "To do so would be pure arbitrariness on my part," Buber responded. "Besides which I do not need to leave the doorway of my ancestral house. The word that is spoken there can be heard on the street." I learned this as I learned that the way to reality is not through some universal but through the particular—the very particular in which one finds oneself in any given time and situation.

So I did not accept what I saw as a very kind and generous offer on Rabbi Greenberg's part—I did not enter the Seminary and settled for teaching Judaism but not practicing it in the Orthodox sense or ever becoming a rabbi. In the summer of 1967 I was the scholar-in-residence at Oconomowoc—a Reform Jewish summer camp in Wisconsin. Since all the other adults at the camp were rabbis, when someone interviewed me for the camp paper, they asked me why I was not a rabbi. "In Tulsa, when I grew up, being a rabbi was not even a live option for me," I replied.

I took two courses in biblical Hebrew at the Oriental Institute of the University of Chicago when I was working on my doctorate.

In the late 1950s I was Chairman of the American Friends of Ihud. IHUD, which means unity, was the Israeli association for Jewish–Arab rapprochement run by Martin Buber and Ernst Simon. One of our active members was Murray (later Moshe) Klebanoff, who stayed in New York City until his mother died, his apartment building was vacated, and his own apartment overrun by rats! At this point he moved to Israel. When my wife Eugenia, our two children David and Dvora, and I were in Jerusalem for seven months in 1966 while I was doing research on what became my three-volume *Martin Buber's Life and Work*, I saw the now highly Orthodox Moshe Klebanoff several times. He told me how he divided his life between study at the Hebrew University and living with the Bratzlaver Hasidim in the Me'a Shearim, or the Hundred Gates—the super, super-orthodox section of Jerusalem—with the result that the Bratzlaver young men would go in his room and burn his university books! When Buber died, said Moshe, they used the Hebrew words customary for the death of an animal! As Buber himself once said, he brought Hasidism to the West against the will of the Hasidim, who did not care about the West and could not forgive Buber for popularizing Hasidism without being orthodox like themselves!

I told Moshe that in the fall of 1966 I would be the first non-Catholic to be professor of philosophy and religion at Manhattanville College of the Sacred Heart in the 140 years of their existence. I also told him that I would be teaching a course on Judaism there. "You should explain to your students that your Judaism is not the real thing," Moshe said to me. "I could do that, Moshe," I said, "but students will always be more influenced by the living presence of the teacher than by any such disclaimers on his part."

Despite my decision not to take up Rabbi Greenberg's generous offer to subsidize my study of Hebrew, for years Dr. Heschel called me up every Sunday morning without fail to ask how my study of Hebrew was coming. Although I studied conversational Hebrew before we went to Israel in 1960 and also at the Hebrew University in Jerusalem, I never mastered Hebrew the way Heschel hoped I would.

2

Man's Quest for Meaning
Heschel and His Disciples

Heschel shared with me his remarkable essay on "Prayer," as he later shared with me everything he wrote in English. He was originally from Poland and wrote a fluent Polish and German before he learned to write English more beautifully and poetically than most persons for whom English was native! Heschel's essay on "Prayer" had a profound impact on me. I remember particularly his story about two towns both of which had clocks but neither of which had a person who repaired clocks. The one town let their clocks run down, as a result of which all their clocks rusted. The other town kept their clocks running, even though they knew that they did not have the right time. At long last a man who repaired clocks showed up in both towns. He was able to repair the clocks of the town that had kept their clocks running but not of the town that had let theirs become inactive and rusted!

Heschel also shared with me what the Sabbath meant to him. "If it were not for the Sabbath," Heschel said to me, "I do not know how I could get through each week." The sense of joy that Heschel found in the Sabbath and in observing the *mitzvoth* was my first introduction to what Heschel later called the "holy dimension" of Jewish deeds. It gave content to what otherwise might have seemed entirely foreign to me.

It was also during this period that I began to come into contact with Heschel's disciples among the rabbinical students at the seminary—Montford Harris, who struck me as a young mystic in his own right, and Hershel Matt, who, under the influence of Heschel and Will Herberg, made the journey from Reconstructionism to an altogether different kind of theology and piety. Today Hershel's son Daniel has become a leading expert on the Kabbala and has received a remarkable grant to translate the *Zohar*, the central text of medieval Jewish mysticism.

Later, when I was studying for my doctorate as a Fellow of the Committee on the History of Culture at the University of Chicago, Heschel regularly sent to see me those of his disciples who lived or studied there—Samuel Dresner and Seymour Siegel in particular. Sam was not so gentle with me on the subject of Halakhah as Heschel was. Though the Jewish law remained a constant question and tension between Heschel and me, he emphatically rejected Sam's assertion of that time that anyone on the other side of the line of the law was not a Jew (i.e. not an authentic Jew). I assumed that Martin Buber was an observant Jew from the fact that he had a beard. Ironically, it was Sam Dresner who informed me that Buber was not observant and thereby relieved me of a part of my tension on the subject.

Heschel himself came to Chicago several times during these years. It was he who told me to read Paul Tillich on religious symbolism, and it was he who encouraged me to continue my study of biblical Hebrew at the Oriental Institute and of modern Hebrew at the College of Jewish Studies in Chicago. Once, I attended a lecture that Heschel gave in Yiddish and found that Heschel spoke such a purely German Yiddish that I understood him through my knowledge of German despite my total ignorance of Yiddish! Another time there was a gathering with Heschel at a home in Northside Chicago I attended along with Everett Gendler, an undergraduate at the University of Chicago whom I had brought into the chapter of the Jewish Peace Fellowship that I had started there. Today Everett Gendler is one of America's leading peace rabbis.

When I received my PhD from the University of Chicago in 1950, Heschel was as proud of me as if I had been his own son. He went over my dissertation and made most helpful suggestions as to how to cut out excess verbiage, tighten, and solidify. "Why should I pay five cents for this word?" Heschel would ask me. I should be able to complete the task of revising it for publication in a year, Heschel advised me. He was quite dismayed when, after my personal contact with Buber, who gave me all sorts of bibliography and advice, I spent four years acquiring and integrating vast amounts of new materials on the implications of Buber's thought for many fields.

It was these four years that issued into my first book *Martin Buber: The Life of Dialogue*. Heschel was pleased with the result and said that my book would certainly last for a generation as the decisive study of Buber's thought. Actually it has lasted a good deal longer than that. In 2001 I received a forwarded message from Routledge in London "to the estate of Maurice Friedman." They assumed that after all this time I must be dead, particularly as they did not know how young I was when my first book was published! I wrote a new Preface to the fourth edition and added two appendices to show Buber's current relevance: "Buber and Emmanuel Levinas," the French philosopher, and "Buber and Mikhail Bakhtin," the Russian literary theorist. But I did not change the text at all, only referring to the third volume of my *Martin Buber's Life and Work* to update Buber's impact on Christian theologians.

When I came to New York City in 1950, Heschel arranged for me to spend a week at the seminary so that I could read the manuscript of his book *Man Is Not Alone: A Philosophy of Religion*. I was fascinated by the way in which he stapled together his aphoristic sentences to produce an organic whole, and I was charmed by the power and the style of his writing. Though Heschel generously credited my help at the back of the book, I am afraid that my responses were disappointing. Instead of the profound philosophical and religious criticisms that he hoped for, I would come up with: *page 66, line 7, semicolon after "prayer"*—a compulsive habit that I have never been able to shake off as the result of the one subject that I ever detested teaching, English composition. Heschel would exclaim in mock admiration, "Wonderful! How did you get your knowledge of English grammar?"

Nonetheless, this was an important week for me, of cementing my friendship with Sam Dresner (sadly, we did not remain friends in the last years of his life) and, through Heschel's arranging it, of spending a Shabbat in Williamsburg, Brooklyn, among the American Hasidim. This last had a great impact on me. In the altogether radiant and spontaneous way in which my Williamsburg host kissed the mezuzah over the door or said the *brachah* (blessing) over the wine and bread at the Shabbat meal, I glimpsed where Heschel found his joy in the Sabbath and in the *mitzvoth*. I was particularly impressed by the experience of sitting in the dark for hours at the Klausenberger Rebbe's synagoge while the Hasidim sang *niggunim* (wordless songs) after sundown on Saturday. On my return I asked Heschel why, if he envied me my weekend there as he repeatedly said, he did not go to live in Williamsburg. "I cannot," he replied. "When I left my home in Poland, I became a modern Western man. I cannot reverse this."

3

The Sabbath
Heschel at Home and in His Study

In the fall of 1951 the Jewish Theological Seminary was the setting of a celebration of Heschel's profound and beautiful little book *The Sabbath*. On the way to the celebration I asked Martin Buber, who had recently arrived in America as a guest of the seminary, if he was going. "I have no time for parties," he answered shortly.

Not long after this, Eugenia and I met Heschel's new wife Sylvia, a lovely woman who had been a concert pianist but gave this up to marry Heschel. At the seminary people joked playing upon Heschel's title *Man Is Not Alone*. Not too long after that Susannah Heschel was born, to the everlasting delight of her parents. I saw her a number of times as a small child and then again as a teenager and as a freshman at Trinity College, where she showed me around when I came there to lecture. She became a lovely woman in her own right, finishing her doctorate in Judaic studies, editing books on Jewish feminism and a collection of works of her father.

In June of 1985, on the occasion of my coming to New York City to receive the National Jewish Book award in Biography for my three-volume *Martin Buber's Life and Work*, I went to see Sylvia Heschel for the first time in years—just twelve years after Heschel himself had died. Lovely as ever in an apartment full of marvelous Heschel pictures, portraits, and mementoes, she played the piano for me and inscribed Heschel's posthumous book *The Circle of the Baal Shem Tov*: "Congratulations on your many important accomplishments that Heschel anticipated on his first meeting with you. In admiration, Sylvia Heschel." I was touched that she remembered those early days of forty years ago as vividly as I did.

Of my visits to Heschel's home, the most memorable was the Passover Seder where Heschel proved himself a true Hasid by eating a two-inch chunk of horseradish and drinking great quantities of schnapps. Not long before that he had come to lecture at Sarah Lawrence College where I was still teaching. Looking at the new Reisinger Auditorium that was the pride of the college, Heschel remarked, "No one will even notice this building in twenty-five years." But then he pointed to the Lawrence mansion at the top of the hill that served as the college's administration building. "Now this will last." While there, he met one of my students who claimed to be a direct descendant of the Baal Shem. When we went in to the Seder, Heschel asked about her. "She was expelled from the college for poor performance in her studies," I responded. This seemed to impress

Heschel, who no doubt wondered whether a progressive women's college like Sarah Lawrence had any standards!

The most frequent setting in which I saw Heschel was the study that he occupied from the time that he came to the seminary until his death. This study was a world of its own with an unbelievable clutter of Hasidic books and manuscripts, Judaica of every description mixed with modern books and a file for the books that Heschel himself was working on.

I was impressed when after many years Heschel got into his study one of those super-comfortable recliner chairs in which he could sit back and smoke his invariable cigar or even take short naps. After Heschel's death, I heard that his Japanese disciple was setting his study in order. It must have been a Herculean feat!

Occasionally too I would walk with Heschel from the seminary to his home on Riverside Drive and stop and have orange juice on the way. Or I would see him at some conference or lecture. Once we were together on Long Island where a group of his disciples met. I gave a little speech of my own. I remarked that ten years before I had wanted to find community by devoting myself to Hasidism, yet I had never been so lonely in my life as I was now. Heschel said that was the first time he had heard me speak.

Heschel and I rode together on the plane to Chicago where he was keynote speaker for the Religious Education Association national convention in which I also took part. I shared with Heschel an article I had written at the request of *Religion and Mental Health* on Jewish social responsibility. "It has no Jewish scholarly content whatsoever," he aptly though not harshly commented.

When I was Visiting Professor of Religious Philosophy at the Hebrew Union College–Jewish Institute of Religion in Cincinnati, I picked up something of how totally isolated and out of place Heschel must have felt himself when he was there thirteen years before when he had just come from London. It is to Hebrew Union College's great credit that it brought Heschel over, undoubtedly saving his life and laying the groundwork for his momentous career in America. But in those days, in some contrast to what it is now, Hebrew Union College was so far removed from what Heschel stood for that they could hardly have had a common language. What is more, the students were especially cruel to Heschel. Someone related to me how Heschel came there to lecture a few years later after he had already moved to the seminary and how totally unsympathetic his audience was. When Heschel left Hebrew Union College for the seminary in 1944, he took with him Samuel Dresner and Richard Rubenstein, both of whom had been students there.

When I was Chairman of the American Friends of Ihud in the late 1960s, I tried in vain to get Heschel to join our really very distinguished board. "I will not join a board that has on it Hans Kohn, a well-known anti-Zionist," commented Heschel. Hans Kohn, a great historian, particularly well known for his work on nationalism and himself author of the first Buber biography, which appeared when Buber was fifty, had gone to Palestine as a Zionist of the Buber persuasion and had become so disillusioned that he left Palestine for America and turned his back on Zionism. I mistakenly thought that Heschel's refusal to join our board meant that Heschel was too concentrated on his studies to be interested in social action. His activities in the sixties and early seventies proved this to be anything but the case.

I once brought Heschel together with one of my own professors from the University of Chicago, the great White-headian philosopher Charles Hartshorne. They found they had much in common both philosophically and spiritually. Another time Heschel showed me an inscription that the sociologist Eugen Rosenstock-Huessy wrote in a book that he gave Heschel: "From the philosopher of times to the philosopher of time." Rosenstock-Huessy's thought was based on a grammar of past, present, and future, Heschel's, particularly in *The Sabbath*, on time as the ever-present, ever-renewed creative event, the medium that encompasses space and gives the reality of holiness to our world.

After I had led two weekends at the Esalen Institute at Big Sur, I followed up a suggestion of Michael Murphy, the President of Esalen Imstitute, and invited Heschel to come to Esalen and do a weekend with me. In my letter to Heschel I extolled Esalen as one of the few places of openness and growth in America. My criticism of some of the atmosphere of Esalen only matured in later years, and I never totally lost the impact of those two early weekends there. Heschel's response was both negative and skeptical. "I get two hundred invitations a year. Why should I accept this one?" he asked me, and I could not reply to his satisfaction.

I early learned in my relationship with Heschel that if he could not speak well of a person, he would not speak at all. One of the things I most admired about Heschel, indeed, was that constant spiritual presence and awareness that warded off every trace of malice and envy and kept far from him idle gossip and personal spite. When I went as visiting professor to Hebrew Union College, Heschel warned me against such gossip; but then added, "But of course you wouldn't." Once Heschel asked me without comment to read a paper given to him by a professor of philosophy at the City College of New York. The paper turned out to be a total plagiarism of my chapter on Martin Buber's theory of knowledge from my book *Martin Buber: The Life of Dialogue*. The student in question—a mature refugee from Europe—was expelled not only from City College but also from the teacher's section of the Jewish Theological Seminary, where he was also enrolled.

The only exception to Heschel's not speaking badly of a person was the great German existentialist philosopher Martin Heidegger, whose Nazi speeches were recorded in a book that Heschel referred me to and that I drew on heavily in my own book *The Worlds of Existentialism*, Guido Schneeberger's *Nachlese zu Heidegger*. Heidegger had withdrawn from his Nazi party activities and his rectorship of Freiburg University in 1934, but he continued to identify himself for some years with its thought (as in his book *Introduction to Metaphysics*) and never, even in his posthumously published interview with *Der Spiegel*, made a real recantation. An American professor who visited Heidegger told Heschel that Heidegger remarked to him that he was sorry that so many Jewish professors managed to make their escape to America. Since the only alternative to this escape was certain death at the hands of the Nazis, we have to assume that this is what Heidegger had in mind for them as, from his point of view, a more acceptable fate!

Heschel went twice to Rome in connection with the Second Vatican Council and two times had audiences with the Pope. His great concern as to the outcome of the council's statement on the Jews that he expressed in letters and in other ways has been well documented. The leading public Quaker, Douglas Steere, humorously told me of the frequent calls that Heschel would make to Steere from Rome. "Douglas," said Steere to me, imitating Heschel's accent, "we must do something about this!" (see chapter 11 below).

I was so timid about bringing up people with Heschel that I never mentioned a Hasidic cousin of his who involved me and quite a number of leading figures in the Jewish academic world in an ambitious scheme to translate and publish Hasidic teachings in a monumental *Corpus Hasidica*. "Why didn't you ask me about him?" Heschel exclaimed when I finally mentioned this debacle after it was all over.

In those days, the 1960s and early 70s, Heschel's voice was often heard on social matters—the Russian Jews, Martin Luther King's marches in the South, race relations in Chicago, old age, and Clergy and Laymen against the War in Vietnam, which Heschel co-chaired with Robert McAfee Brown. I was never more proud of Heschel than when he wrote a truly prophetic letter to *The New York Times* asking what Amos would say about corruption in the very highest places. This letter was prophetic in the real sense of the prophetic demand for justice and in the popular sense of proclaiming the corruption a few months before Watergate broke!

Heschel's dream for me I never fulfilled—that of acquiring a thorough knowledge of Hebrew and making the contribution to Jewish learning and religious thought that he felt I could make. With great and gentle patience he often used to call me up on Sunday mornings during the years I lived near New York City asking me about how my study of Hebrew was progressing. If my answer did not satisfy him, neither did he give up hope for me during all those years.

Thus a pattern was set in our relationship that persisted to the end—that of great affection and friendship on both sides and, on my side, near but never full discipleship. Loyalty, gratitude to, and admiration for him were always coupled with my holding my own position—in some significant ways at variance with his. This tension was always contained without our friendship ever knowing a real conflict or serious strain.

That I was never able to follow *Halakhah*—the "Way of deeds"—was as great a disappointment to Heschel as my failure to follow my own goal of really mastering Hebrew and studying midrashic and Hasidic texts with him. Yet neither of these disappointments ever affected his friendship for me. Even when I moved to Philadelphia as Professor of Religion at Temple University, he periodically called me up and asked me to visit him, which I did on my infrequent visits to New York.

One person of whom Heschel and I frequently spoke was Martin Buber. We shared a deep friendship with Buber—Heschel from his close association with Buber during his years in Germany, myself from a much later period in Buber's life. Once, during Buber's first visit to America in 1951, my wife Eugenia stopped in to see Heschel at the Jewish Theological Seminary in New York and came upon the two men looking so earnestly at each other across Heschel's desk that she retreated without making her presence known. When Heschel heard Gershom Scholem's criticism of Buber in a public lecture, he remarked to me, "You know there is much in Buber's interpretation of Hasidism and Judaism that I cannot accept. But how can Scholem speak against him thus? We have no one like him in world Jewry." Still I think that a third disappointment in Heschel's relationship with me was that I became Buber's disciple to the extent that I did. Heschel wanted me for a fuller life of Jewish praxis. Yet Heschel once remarked to me that every person has some point of reference, some 'touchstone of reality,' to use my own phrase. For me, he knew, it was Hasidism.

My writings on Heschel's thought have been highly appreciative, but they also have contained criticisms, some of which derived from my immersion in Buber's philosophy of dialogue. Once, when I had put into a review article on Heschel's book *The Prophets* a contrast between Heschel's and Buber's treatment of the prophet Hosea, Heschel asked me as a personal favor to take it out so that he would not be obliged to write a public criticism of Buber—something he had never done. On the other hand, he took a lively interest in the critical biography of Buber that I was writing and freely offered me whatever recollections and suggestions he could. The years in Nazi Germany were the period of Buber's true greatness, Heschel stressed; for great as his books were, Buber was greater still as a man, especially at the time of his people's most terrible agony.

One field is the most that any man can master, Heschel once observed to me, but Buber mastered two fields—the Bible and Hasidism. Heschel suggested to me that I should take some of Buber's letters to a handwriting expert to see what his handwriting told about his personality. I never did, but the idea intrigued me. Once when I criticized Heschel's comments on Buber's I–Thou philosophy, Heschel gave me a pained look and said, "Do you think I don't understand Buber?"

In a statement he gave my editor at Dutton, Heschel described my book *Touchstones of Reality* as "a deeply moving account of the pilgrimage of a sensitive and rich soul, the ingathering of a vast amount of wonderful insights." Heschel said to me, in fact, that *Touchstones of Reality*, which combines early autobiography with my dialogue with some of the world's great religions, should have been titled "The Pilgrimage of a Soul."

Heschel read and commented on all my books. He also made suggestions concerning the English original and the Hebrew translation of the monograph "Divine Need and Human Wonder: The Philosophy of Abraham Joshua Heschel" that I wrote for the second volume of *Brit Ivrit Olamit*'s three-volume Israeli Publication *Spiritual Contributions of American Jews*. Heschel told me rather humorously that my essay read better in the Hebrew translation than in the English original! Despite my occasional criticisms, he seemed very pleased that it would appear. My last contact with him was on the subject of this essay, which I wrote as an act of personal devotion to him.

Part Two

Heschel and Hasidism

4

The Circle of the Baal Shem Tov
The Scion of Hasidism

It was many years before I understood how ludicrous was my idea that I could regenerate American Hasidism and how kind Heschel was in accepting me rather than rejecting me outright! To help the reader understand this aspect of my friendship with and relationship to Heschel I must speak here of Heschel's Hasidic childhood and of Heschel's continuing relationship to Hasidism throughout his life.

Abraham Joshua Heschel was born in Warsaw, Poland, in 1907. His childhood grounded him deeply in the world of the Hasidim, the popular communal Jewish mystics of Eastern Europe. He was descended on his father's side from Dov Baer, the Maggid of Mezeritch, the successor to the Baal Shem Tov, and from his own namesake Avraham Yehoshua Heschel of Apt, the Apter Rebbe. On his mother's side he was descended from the great Hasidic rabbi Levi Yitzhak of Berditchev. Heschel's disciple Samuel H. Dresner gives us a glimpse of Heschel's Hasidic childhood in his introduction to Heschel's posthumous book *The Circle of the Baal Shem Tov*:

> From Heschel's childhood on, there were Hasidic leaders who looked to him as one with unique promise for renewing Hasidic life . . . Descended from Hasidic nobility on both his father's and his mother's side, young Heschel's talents were early recognized and, though he was only a child of ten at the time of his father's death, the Hasidim began to bring him k'vitlakh and wished him to become their Rebbe. "We thought," said the Rebbe of Kopitchnitz, a cousin and brother-in-law, "that he would be the Levi Yitzhak of our generation." A byword after his departure was that "had Heschel become a Rebbe, all the other Rebbim would have lost their Hasidim."
>
> But the awareness of the worlds "outside" was stirring and the young Heschel did not accede to the Hasidim's wishes. His interest in secular studies began at about the age of fifteen or sixteen. His decision to leave Warsaw for Vilna and, later, Berlin to gain a secular education was received with concern.
>
> He claimed that he was no longer a Hasid. He had, indeed, abandoned their style of dress and of restricted social contacts for the larger world, both Jewish and German.[1]

Heschel left Poland at twenty to study philosophy at the University of Berlin, from which he received his PhD in 1937. He also studied Semitics and was an instructor in Talmud at the famous Hochschule für die Wissenschaft des Judentums. In 1937 he was chosen by Martin Buber as his successor at the Central Organization for Jewish Adult

1. Dresner, *Heschel, Hasidism and Halakha*, 61.

Education and as the director of the Freie Jüdische Leh-rhaus at Frankfurt.

Studying philosophy at the University of Berlin, He-schel became increasingly aware of the gulf that separated his views from those of his professors and fellow students. They spoke of God from the point of view of man, whereas to Heschel the Torah was a vision of man from the point of view of God. They were concerned with how to be good. Heschel was concerned with how to be holy. Prisoners of a Greek-German way of thinking, they were fettered in categories presupposing metaphysical assumptions that could never be proved.

Discovering that values sweet to taste proved sour in analysis, Heschel went through moments of profound bitterness and loneliness. Then, walking alone through the streets of Berlin, Heschel became aware one evening that the sun had gone down and that he had not said the evening prayer. Although his heart was heavy and his soul was sad, he rediscovered his task that evening—"to restore the world to the kingship of the Lord."[2]

Expelled by the Nazis in 1938, Heschel taught for eight months at the Institute for Jewish Studies in Warsaw. Then he was fortunate enough to get to London where he established the Institute for Jewish Learning. He was brought to America by the Hebrew Union College–Jewish Institute of Religion and from 1940 to 1945 was Associate Professor of Philosophy and Rabbinics in Cincinnati, Ohio. In 1945 he moved to New York to become Professor of Jewish Ethics and Mysticism at the Jewish Theological

2. Quoted in ibid., 9.

Seminary, where he remained all the rest of his life except for a year as the Harry Emerson Fosdick Visiting Professor at Union Theological Seminary, New York City.

Heschel saw Hasidism neither as a sect nor as a doctrine, but as a dynamic approach to reality that succeeded in liquifying a frozen system of values and ideas. The Hasid studied the Talmud to experience its soul and to envision worlds. Hasidism set life aflame: it brought warmth, light, enthusiasm. Stressing truthfulness and wholeheartedness, Hasidism placed the aphorism and the parable at the center of Hasidic thinking and transformed doctrines into attitudes and facts.

All this was embodied as never before or since in the founder of Hasidism—Israel ben Eliezer (1700–1760), who came to be known as the Baal Shem Tov, the good master of the name of God, or, shortened, the Besht. The unbelievable impact that the Besht had in such a short time is explained by Heschel through the fact that, while many Jews talked about God, it was the Besht who brought God to the people.

> He who really wants to be uplifted by communing with a great person whom he can love without reservation, who can enrich his thought and imagination without end, that person can meditate about the life . . . of the Besht. There has been no one like him during the last thousand years.[3]

> Descendant of a Hasidic dynasty [writes Samuel Dresner] and heir of the living tradition at its most vital source, master of the philosophical and historical-critical method of the West as well as possessing unusual creative gifts, Heschel was

3. Heschel, *Moral Grandeur and Spiritual Audacity*, 34.

perhaps the one scholar who might have given us the definitive work on Hasidism.[4]

Hasidism, Heschel asserted, is essentially an oral
movement that cannot be preserved in written form, a
living movement that is not contained fully in any of its
books. "To be a Hasid is to be in love with God and with
what God has created." If you have never been in love in
this way, you will not understand the history of Hasidism
and may consider it a madness. Asserting that Judaism is
today in need of repair, Heschel labeled the great Hasidim
"the repair men of the Holy of Holies." In the Hasidic
movement the spirit was alive in the word as a voice, not
a mere idea. Its words have the power to repair, to revive,
to create, if one learns how to be perceptive to the voice
within them. Its words still ring with the passion and enthusiasm of those who spoke them. "The problem is how
to hear the voice through the words." In many Hasidic
books God's presence is felt on every page.

Heschel's Hasidic understanding went far beyond
books, of course. Due to his early upbringing, he possessed
a remarkable sensitivity to the core of Hasidic authenticity
as it was transmitted from generation to generation. As a
result, Heschel stressed that Hasidism can never be understood on the basis of literary sources alone without drawing
upon the oral tradition which preserves its authentic living
source. Translated often unsuccessfully from Yiddish into
Hebrew, Hasidic literature can never in itself make up for
listening to the living tongue of the masters and standing

4 Dresner, *Heschel, Hasidism and Halakha*, 75.

close to Hasidic personages. This Heschel could do as none of those who followed him could hope to emulate.

In his childhood and youth Heschel lived in the presence of quite a number of extraordinary persons he could revere, and their presence continued to live in him as an adult. Above all, he retained the capacity to be surprised at life—a capacity that he saw as the supreme Hasidic imperative. Shlomo Beillis, from the circle of Yiddish poets to which Heschel belonged when he studied at the gymnasium in Vilna, describes how Heschel would surprise him by bringing along his dark hat when they took walks through the forest and, upon entering the woods, would put it on. "When I inquired for the reason, he replied in his soft voice: 'I don't know if you will understand. To me a forest is a holy place, and a Jew does not enter a holy place without covering his head!'"

In his emphasis upon the oral as opposed to the written, Heschel is close to Martin Buber. Heschel was also close to Buber in his recognition that there were *two* streams that came forth from Hasidism, and not one, as both Gershom Scholem and his disciple Rivka Schatz-Uffenheimer maintain—that of the hallowing of the everyday, which began with the Baal Shem, and that of the Gnostic nullifying of the particular in favor of the transcendent, which began with the Baal Shem's successor, Dov Baer, the Maggid of Mezeritch. This contrast emerges with great clarity in Heschel's essay on the Baal Shem's friend R. Pinchas of Korzec (or Koretz). In this essay, writes Dresner, Heschel "delineated the ideological conflict which occurred early in the history of the movement, in which each side claimed that it possesses the true meaning of the Besht's legacy":

The maggid of Miedzyrzecz [Mezeritch] had stressed the centrality of Kabbalah and established *devekut* as the highest goal. For him, the awareness that all is God would lead man to understand that this world is but so many veils which must be cast aside to enter into the divine embrace. The maggid's language is strongly Lurianic, with spiritual ascent beyond time and place the all-consuming goal. For R. Pinhas, on the other hand, the stress is elsewhere. This world is no illusion. It is the place, and now is the time, where man must labor diligently and unremittingly to perfect himself. To escape the world is to violate the Psalmist's admonition that one must first "turn from evil" and only then "do good." . . . R. Pinhas emphasized moral virtue and simple faith.

The Maggid introduced the methods of the Lurianic Kabbalah into the teaching of the Besht—*kavanot* and *yihudim* (special mystical intentions and exercises), *devekut* (cleaving to God), and *hitlahavut* (burning enthusiasm, or ecstasy). His disciple Shneur Zalman taught that the essence of all things was intellectual contemplation on the greatness of God. Rabbi Pinchas, in contrast, criticized those who wanted to learn the secrets of the Torah and to achieve lofty rungs of insight. He preferred unquestioning simplicity, honesty, and humility to *yihudim* and *kavanot*. "The battle between these two forms of Hasidim—the one, scholarly, speculative, and aristocratic; the other, that of the Ukrainian tzaddikim, poetic, moralistic, and popular—continued for generations." The maggid of Mezeritch and many of his followers, such as Levi Yitzhak of Berditchev, believed that true prayer demanded *hitlahavut* and that *hitlahavut* demanded various kinds of special preparations.

Rabbi Pinhas did not hold with special preparations for prayer nor with praying with excessive vigor and in a loud voice.

5

A Passion for Truth
Between the Baal Shem
and the Kotzker Rebbe

Much in my thirty years of personal friendship and dialogue with Abraham Heschel was clarified when I read his posthumous book *A Passion for Truth* and particularly its introduction, "Why I Had to Write This Book," which also served as the introduction for his much larger Yiddish book *Kotsk: In Gerangle far Emes Dikeyt* [Kotzk: The Struggle in Integrity]. This introduction showed Heschel as living his whole life in the tension between the positive life affirmation of Israel ben Eliezer (1700–1760), the Baal Shem Tov, who was the founder of Hasidism, and a zaddik, or Hasidic rebbe, of the sixth generation of zaddikim, Rabbi Menahem Mendel of Kotzk (1787–1859). Heschel's childhood was spent in the atmosphere of Mezbizh, which preserved the memory not only of its last great rebbe, his namesake, the Apter Rebbe, but also of the Baal Shem. The parables of the Baal Shem that Heschel thus learned made the Besht a "model too sublime to follow, yet too overwhelming to ignore"; whereas the Kotzker Rebbe, about whom he learned in his ninth year, haunted and often stunted him, urging him to confront perplexities that he might otherwise have passed unnoticed. Thus his soul was at home with the Baal Shem but driven by the Kotzker, torn between the joy of the one and the anxiety of the other.

No one understands Heschel who imagines his writings to be a mere outpouring of devotional piety. If his heart was in Mezbizh, his mind was in Kotzk. If he kept the link with the centuries of Jewish faith through the "mines of Meaning" inherited from the Baal Shem, he also kept the link with the modern world through the "immense mountains of absurdity" placed in his way by the model of Kotzk. "The one taught me song, the other silence."[1] If the former imparted to him compassion and mercy and made his dark hours luminous, the latter eased wretchedness and desolation by forewarnings and premonitions of Auschwitz. (Elie Wiesel points out in Souls on Fire that the Kotzker Rebbe went into his twenty years of self-enforced seclusion just one hundred years before the outbreak of the Second World War.) "The Baal Shem dwelled in my life like a lamp, while the Kotzker struck like lightning."[2] The Kotzker debunked cherished attitudes and warned of the peril of forfeiting authenticity, even while the Baal Shem helped Heschel refine his sense of immediate mystery and gave him the gift of elasticity in adapting to contradirtory

1. Heschel, A Passion for Truth, xiv.
2. Ibid., xv.

conditions. "The Baal Shem gave me wings, the Kotzker encircled me with chains. I never had the courage to break the chains, and entered into joys with my shortcomings in mind. I owe intoxication to the Baal Shem to the Kotzker the blessings of humiliation."[3]

These contrasts are continued in the body of *A Passion for Truth* itself, and as such they establish the link between one of the most remarkable religious lives of the twentieth century and the philosophy of religion which that life produced. The Baal Shem emphasized love, joy, and compassion for this world, all of which Heschel shared, but the Kotzker demanded constant tension, which Heschel also shared. "The passionate indignation of the Prophets came back to life in the Kotzker." In Abraham Heschel the Baal Shem's realization that "the world is full of enormous lights and mysteries which man shuts from himself with one small hand" led directly to an equally passionate prophetic indignation based not upon the Kotzker's harshness but upon sympathy with God's own indignation at the treatment of the wretched and the poor!

At the beginning of my book *The Hidden Human Image*, I tell of the Hasidim who once told stories of the Baal Shem and lamented, "Alas, where could we find such a man today?" Exclaimed their rebbe, "Fools, he is present in every generation, only then he was manifest, now he is hidden." This tale points, I suggest, to "the unmanifest, hidden, imageless yet present, authentic man of today." It is exactly in this spirit that Heschel wrote *A Passion for Truth* and celebrated in it, at first subtly then ever more

3. Ibid.

powerfully, the Kotzker's insistence *and his own* that Truth lies buried, stifled in the grave, yet still remains alive. "Truth is homeless in our world. We suffocate for lack of honesty. As a result, man dies while yet alive. Who can speak of resurrection when life itself has become death? Coarse and swaggering, men make insolent speeches and engage in presumptuous dealings. But they are dead, while Truth, though muted in the grave, is alive."

Heschel did not share in the Kotzker's enmity to this world. The distinction between the righteous and the wicked is that "the wicked are trapped by material things that bring them pleasure," whereas "the righteous are enhanced by the mystery of the Divine inherent in things. Their wonder sustains their lives." This wonder became for Heschel the root of all knowledge and of all meaningful living. In this he remained the disciple of the Baal Shem, who emphasized God's nearness and saw his distance as a game that a father plays with his child. Mendel was profoundly opposed to the Baal Shem's conception of the world infused with the Divine; for, like the prophet, he saw the heart as deceitful above all things and desperately corrupt (Jeremiah 17:9). God dwells in the world, said Mendel, only where man lets Him in. In Heschel wonder and prophetic indignation, the apprehension of the divine in everything and the lamentation at how man shuts out the divine by his insensitiveness, were two sides of the same coin.

For Heschel, as for the Kotzker and his own master the Holy Yehudi (Jew), Truth was not a doctrine or a metaphysic but integrity of personal existence. What the Baal Shem and the Kotzker treated as an either/or, Heschel somehow combined: for the former love and compassion were higher than truth; for the latter a man's love and goodness were shame if he himself was false. Heschel demanded compassion and truth together. Both have for him a single source: the awareness of the ineffable. Yet the tension remains—in *A Passion for Truth* and in Heschel himself.

Heschel ends with the astounding, and to me almost unbelievable, conclusion that despite the awe the Kotzker's thoughts evoke, "he cannot serve as a model. For it is surely not the will of God that man lead a tortured life." It is true that Heschel followed the Baal Shem in emphasizing joy, but that joy was in no way incompatible for him with the terrible anguish of being one of the very few to be embarrassed by the man of his day! I would not, indeed, say of Heschel what he said of Kierkegaard and the Kotzker, namely, that both may have been afflicted with mental illness and that some of their thinking may have been conditioned by it. Yet Heschel's embarrassment at the low state to which man has fallen in our day enabled him equally with them "to see through the falsehood of society and to come upon the burial place where Truth is entombed."

The personal illness of the nineteenth century has been succeeded by the massive social illness of the twentieth, and it is for this reason that Heschel can recognize, as few others, the special relevance of both Kierkegaard and the Kotzker "today in exposing dishonesty as the disease underlying the political and social life of the modern world," a retrospective judgment illuminated by the Nazi Holocaust and the dreaded nuclear age! Otherwise, how could we explain the pathos with which Heschel recounts the withdrawal of the Kotzker Rebbe during the last twenty years of his life: "His voice remained enveloped in darkness like a wind howling in the night. Yet some people will feel smitten some day, for those who ran away did not let him finish what he had to say . . . the Kotker did not fail. He may have thought he had little impact, but the struggle he waged goes on; his words once again act as a battle cry."

It is in the *contrasts* that Heschel makes between Kierkegaard and the Kotzker that we can see how closely Heschel identifies lumself with the latter. The Kotzker's "agony reached a limit in dssmay, not in despair. He was baffled, not shattered. His misery defied explanation, yet it was not beyond hope or cure." No more exact description could be made of Heschel himself. The Kotzker stressed conflict and opposition as well as analogy and cooperation between God and man. "He insisted upon the importance of both human enterprise and divine assistance, human initiative and divine grace." This biblically Jewish emphasis upon the primordial dialogue between God and man issues, in the Kotzker and in Heschel, into Job's protest against God's injustice, "the awareness that God was ultimately responsible for the hideousness of human mendacity." What concerned the Kotzker was the paradox of divine responsibility, *the myth of the buried Truth*, rather than that of fallen man, as with Kierkegaard. In the midst of this Jobian anguish, Heschel inserts his own witness to the "mysterious waiting which every human being senses at moments: something is being asked of me." This, too, is a fundamentally dialogical witness: "Meaning is found in understanding the demand and in responding to it." Levi Yitzhak of Berditchev does not pray that God show him the secret of His divine ways but that He show him ever more clearly what this event that is happening to him demands of him, "what you Lord of the world are asking me by way of it."

It is not surprising, in the light of all this, that Heschel devotes a whole section *of A Passion for Truth* to "The Kotzker and Job" and that he adds in a footnote on the title page of that section: "This chapter is not an exposition of the Kotzker's view but, rather, an essay on a major problem of faith which is guided by his sayings." "The dialogical leads inevitably to Job's question to God," Martin Buber has written, and Heschel's dialogical philosophy of religion equally leads him to the protest against the injustice of the world. The Kotzker demanded that man confront the heavens and storm them, and Heschel adds his voice to this complaint: "In the Jew of our time, distress at God's predicament may be a more powerful witness than tacit acceptance of evil as inevitable. The outcry of anguish certainly adds more to His glory than callousness or even flattery of the God of pathos."

In utter contrast to Kierkegaard, the Kotzker and Heschel insist that man should never capitulate, not even to the Lord. Both were repelled by submission and blind obedience. "A man must he a rebel in his very existence . . . Even in defeat, continued courage was essential." Some forms of suffering must be accepted with love and borne in silence. To other agonies one must say no. In *The Hidden Human Image* and my 1987 book on Heschel and Wiesel, I point to Elie Wiesel as a "Job of Auschwitz" who carries on in our day the trust and contending of the modern Job. Nothing sounds more exactly like Wiesel than this saying of the Kotzker, which Heschel also makes his own: "Three ways are open to a man who is in sorrow. He who stands on a normal rung weeps, he who stands higher is silent, but he who stands on the topmost rung converts his sorrow into song."

For all this, there is an affirmation in Heschel that goes beyond the Kotzker, beyond Elie Wiesel, and beyond even the meaning that I point to in *To Deny Our Nothingness* in my metaphor of the "Dialogue with the Absurd." Heschel finds a meaning beyond absurdity and above reason: "The complete failure of all consolation, the love of life despite its absurdity, holds out the certainty of a meaning that transcends our understanding. We encounter meaning beyond absurdity in living as a response to an expectation. Expectation of "meaning is an a priori condition of our existence."

At this point the Baal Shem gains the upper hand over the Kotzker: "Our very existence exposes us to the challenge of wonder and radical amazement at the universe despite the absurdities we encounter . . . We are not the final arbiter of meaning. What looks absurd within the limit of time may be luminous within the scope of eternity." *This is* the dominant note that is found in most of Heschel's philosophy of religion, and the Kotzker remains like an underground current to surface passionately at times in a passage on the prophets or on the paradox of "Who is man?"

Heschel does not leave this contradiction, or paradox, totally unresolved. Rather, he recognizes, again in true dialogical fashion, that the growing awareness of history's tragic predicament gives birth to an intuition that man is co-responsible with God, that God needs man, that the problem of the justification of God cannot be separated from that of the justification of man. God does not need those who praise Him when in a state of euphoria but those who are in love with Him even when in distress. God needs man to believe in Him in spite of Him, to continue being a witness despite God's hiding Himself. God needs those who can turn a curse into a blessing, agony into a song, who can go through hell and continue to trust in God's goodness. Faith is the beginning of compassion for God. "It is when bursting with God's sighs that we are touched by the awareness that *beyond all absurdity* there is meaning, Truth, and love."

It is precisely this position that leads Heschel in his conclusion to "The Kotzker Today," to a position significantly at variance with the Kotzker: "The Divine and the human are not by nature conceived to be at odds or in constant tension. Man is capable of acting in accord with God; he is able to be His Partner in redemption, to imitate Him in acts of love and compassion." Yet the final emphasis of the book belongs to the Kotzker—the recognition that it took generations of lies to produce the Holocaust, that Truth is alive, dwelling somewhere, never weary, and all of mankind is needed to liberate it. "In a world that contains so much sham, the Kotzker continues to stand before us as a soul aflame with passion for God, determined to let nothing stand between him and his Maker. In the nineteenth century he was a towering figure, in solitary misery as in grandeur. Yet his spirit, his accent are those of the post-Auschwitz era."

Part Two: Heschel and Hasidism

In the twentieth century Heschel, too, was a towering figure, in anguish and in joy, and his accents are equally those of the Bible, the Talmud, the Hasidim, the Job of Auschwitz, and the terrified inheritors of the nuclear age!

Part Three

Our Dialogue

6

The Earth Is the Lord's

The first book of Heschel's that was published in English was *The Earth Is the Lord's*—a short, non-scholarly story of East European Jewry, to which Heschel was greatly devoted, as was natural from his background. It was illustrated by the artist Ilya Schor who succeeded in creating wonderful pictures that matched Heschel's spirit and his style and fit in well with Heschel's beloved Hasidism. Heschel, as we have seen, was the scion of eight generations of Hasidim back to the great Dov Baer, the Maggid of Mezritch who succeeded Israel ben Eliezer (1700–1760), the founder of Hasidism. Dov Baer wrote down Hasidic teachings and sent out his disciples to organize the communities of Eastern Europe.

Even as a young man Heschel was considered the *zaddik* of his generation, which his faithful American disciple Samuel Dresner later called him.

In *The Sabbath*, also printed before his major theological works, Heschel contrasts the Jewish view that space is contained in time with the more common view that time is contained in space. "It is the world of space which is rolling through the infinite expanse of time." The world of space is constantly perishing while time, through which it moves, is everlasting. The things of space, which ordinarily dominate our vision of the world, conceal the Creator through their deceptive appearance of independence and permanence. Time, on the other hand, reveals the Creator, for through it we intuit the process of creation. "It is the dimension of time wherein man meets God, wherein man becomes aware that every instant is an act of creation, a Beginning, opening up new roads for ultimate realizations. Time is the presence of God in the world of space."[1] We are called upon to sanctify our life in time rather than to sanctify the symbols of space; for the source of time is eternity. The secret of the world's coming into being is the presence of the giver in the given. "To the spiritual eye space is frozen time, and all things are petrified events."[2]

This centrality of time informs all of Heschel's writings. In *God in Search of Man* Heschel contrasts the tendency to look on history as unbroken process with the biblical understanding of history as event, hence as a creative breakthrough of presentness, discontinuous and just for that reason ever in need of being remembered and renewed. In *The Prophets* Heschel shows the "divine pathos" as bound to the events of history and the prophets' "sympathy" with that pathos as a response to and judgment of the events of their time.

History is not the dead past but the ever-renewed present—the burning bush in which each instant vanishes

1. Heschel, *The Sabbath*, 100.
2. Ibid., 97.

to open the way to the next one; yet history itself is not consumed. Heschel boldly names the people of Israel God's stake in human history—not that politics can properly be theologized but that here and there, in seeming disarray, are events that can be gathered to "comprehend the unity of disconnected chords." There can be no material sphere forever cut off from a spiritual one but only the endless task of endowing the material with the radiance of the spirit, sanctifying the common, and sensing the marvelousness of the everyday. Reality is not above time and the concrete, but in them. "The agony of our people particularly in this century was dreadfully concrete and redemption of our people and all peoples must also be concrete." The real is not the heavenly and the eternal as opposed to the earthly and temporary but the deeper unity of both.

"Our interest [in great events]," writes Heschel, "endures long after they are gone . . . The past does not altogether vanish. Some events, hoary with antiquity, may hold us to this present day."[3] "The incidents recorded in the Bible to the discerning eye are episodes of one great drama: the quest of God for man; His search for man, and man's flight from Him."[4]

3. Heschel, *God in Search of Man*, 211.
4. Ibid., 197.

7

Man Is Not Alone
A Philosophy of Religion

When I was asked to review Heschel's *Man Is Not Alone* for *The Journal of Religion*, I spent a week reimmersing myself in it and working out the logical links between the seemingly lyrical passages. This was my first book review, and I spent more time and effort on it than I did later on the many articles that I wrote! I discovered how very difficult it is to retain the full richness of Heschel's poetic imagery and devotional depth and at the same time follow the interconnections of his philosophy of religion. A distinguished literary critic has suggested that a poem falls short if has too much imagery or too much connected thought. Borrowing from that critic's criteria for poetry, I found out that Heschel's poetic writing falls short in that it has more imagery than it has connected thought. This makes it almost impossible for most readers to grasp the connections of his thought.

Nonetheless, my intensive study has confirmed my feeling that Heschel is a highly original and profound philosopher of religion. Heschel had many—both liberal and Orthodox—detractors after the publication of *Man Is Not Alone*. I later answered these detractors in *Congress Weekly*. This was my first article on Heschel's thought—an article that Heschel himself asked me to write.

In *Man Is Not Alone*, writes Arthur A. Cohen, Heschel created a climate of religious ecstasy for those already committed." In my article in *Congress Weekly* I defend Heschel's book from such criticisms. My earlier immersion in the literature and practice of mysticism helped me to do this. *Man Is Not Alone* has as much power to speak to the uncommitted as any book that American thought has produced. The atmosphere of the style, to be sure, breathes faith rather than skepticism, wonder rather than rational doubt. But the faithfulness in the first instance is to the wonder itself. Thus it becomes a fitting instrument for conveying new meaning to the minds of the "uncommitted" who cannot grasp new meaning through abstract concepts but only through full-bodied symbols in which the intellectual is integrated with the intuitive and the emotional. To the "convinced" the abstract concept is sometimes adequate since he or she understands to what it refers, but to the uncommitted such shortcuts are not possible. Heschel appeals to those who "want to taste the whole wheat of the spirit before it is ground by the millstones or reason."

Heschel offers an insight into religious experience that may aid us in attaining a real personal relationship to our religion. Heschel's philosophy of religion does not begin with dogma or the law or with recapitulation of classic proofs of the existence of God, but with that sense of wonder and the ineffable that belongs, in greater or lesser measure, to every person's experience, even though our normal consciousness is in a state of stupor in which our sensibility of the wholly real is radically reduced. Only after we have attained the awareness of the ineffable do we reach that transcendence to which each finite thing alludes through its unique and non-repeatable reality.

Liberals, such as Eugene Borowitz, have sometimes been cut off from a serious encounter with Heschel's thought by the labels that have been attached to it—"poetic," "mystical," "irrational." Actually, Heschel's thought is more rational than most philosophies of religion in its awareness of the special approach that religion demands for understanding—the "situational thinking" and "depth theology" that endeavor to discover the questions to which religion is an answer.

The antagonism to Heschel's thought that one occasionally encounters often seems to be motivated by an uncritical faith in the absoluteness of "reason" as the true basis of religion and a fear of any attitude or way of thinking that might move religion off this secure foundation! The scientist regards his scientific thinking as a tool not a metaphysic. He is content if it solves the problems that he sets or suggests hypotheses that might lead to new problems. The modern scientist would be the first to agree with Heschel's statement that "the world as scrutinized and depicted by science is but a thin surface of undisclosed depths."[1]

"It is not the Psalmist, Rabbi Jehuda Halevy, Rabbi Isaiah Horovitz, or Rabbi Nahman of Bratzlav," Heschel has remarked, "it is Hegel, Freud, or Dewey who has become our guide in matters of Jewish prayer and God."[2] Study, to be sure, has been honored in Judaism for millennia. Not study for its own sake, however, but study of God's revelation in the Torah, that presupposes a prior meeting between God and the human through which that revelation took place. When Moses received God's word on Mount Sinai and the people responded, "We will do and we will hear," it was not reason that came into play but a genuine commitment. If we cannot make this same commitment today, let us have the honesty to say so rather than read back into the Jewish tradition a worship of reason that derives not from the Talmud but from the intellectual climate of modern Western culture and from the Greek and Renaissance thought in which that culture is rooted.

For all its poetic quality, Heschel's style is always an instrument of his thought. The startling combination of words brings new insights to light and forces us beyond the hackneyed to that sense of wonder and awareness of the ineffable that, to Heschel, is the first major step in religious life and thought. His style also helps us retain this awareness, for, as he writes, "Even when our thoughts about the ultimate take place on the discursive level, our memory remains moored in our perceptions of the ineffable . . ."[3]

1. Heschel, *Moral Grandeur and Spiritual Audacity*, 14.
2. Ibid., 109.
3. Heschel, *Man Is Not Alone*, 60.

Heschel does not disparage knowledge and reason. He recognizes, as most philosophers do, that they are not ultimate, that they rest on intuitions, attitudes, and assumptions that cannot be subjected to proof. "The tree of knowledge grows on the soil of mystery."[4] Wonder rather than doubt is the root of philosophy, for the sense of the ineffable alone leads us to meaning—meaning that can never be fully expressed, only indicated.

A distinguished Reform rabbi scornfully dismissed *Man Is Not Alone* as just "another back to God book." For us, he continued, it is "logic and the laboratory" that give us religious certainty. In explicit contradiction to this, Heschel writes that it is not through logic and reason that we come to know God, but through the awareness of the ineffable. Insights into the ineffable are "the roots of man's creative activities in art, thought and noble living."[5] It is radical amazement at what is, the distinction between what may be uttered and what is unutterable that most distinguishes man from the animals. We encounter the ineffable as a powerful presence outside us, a spiritual suggestiveness of reality that gives us certainty without any knowledge that can be detached and abstracted. The ineffable is the something more in all things that gives them transcendent significance. It is an awareness of all being that teaches us that "to be is to stand for."[6] From the hiddenness of things, we come to "the mystery of our own presence" and learn that the self also is not something we own but something transcendent in disguise.

4. Ibid., 7.
5. Heschel, *God in Search of Man*, 39.
6. Ibid., 413.

The awareness of the ineffable is not an aesthetic experience in which one may rest. It is a question that God asks of us and that question and our response are the beginning of religion. Thus through wonder we come to the awareness of God in which "the inexpressible within us to commune with the ineffable beyond us."[7]

God, to Heschel, is One, and "one" means not just the only God, but unique, incomparable, indivisible." One means that God is alone truly real, uniting mercy and law, that He is within us and within all things. "God means: *Togetherness of all beings in holy otherness*."[8]

This does not mean that all is God or that all is one. Heschel's philosophy is not a pantheism but a panentheism in which God and man work together to bring about the unification of God and the world. Evil is divergence and confusion, that which divides man from man and man from God, "while good is *convergence*, togetherness, *union*."[9] God is striving to become one with the world, his transcendent essence is striving to become one with his imminent presence, his *Shekinah*. There is here no radical dualism of good and evil, natural and supernatural. In responding to God we find him near to us. The world is not cut off from God, for his presence lingers, and through this presence we may sanctify all physical life and take it to the beyond. "It is His otherness, ineffable and immediate

7. Heschel, *Moral Grandeur and Spiritual Audacity*, 140.

8. Heschel, *Man Is Not Alone*, 109.

9. Ibid., 120.

as the air we breathe and do not see, which enables us to sense His distant nearness."[10]

"One of the maladies of our time," writes Heschel, "is shattered confidence in human nature."[11] We are inclined to believe that the world is a pandemonium, that there is no sense in virtue, no import in integrity. that we only graft goodness upon selfishness and relish self-indulgence in all values, that we cannot but violate truth with evasion. Honesty is held to be wishful thinking, purity the squaring of the circle of human nature. The hysteria of suspicion has made us unreliable to ourselves, trusting neither our inspirations nor our convictions. Suspiciousness, not skepticism is the beginning of our thinking.

The modern person "has failed to pick up in his youth the unbroken thread of truthfulness that would guide him through the labyrinth."[12]

10. Ibid., 122.

11. Heschel, *Moral Grandeur and Spiritual Audacity*, 6.

12. Ibid.

8

Critical Questions for Heschel

I found myself following the development of Heschel's philosophy of religion and his philosophy of Judaism with each new book, working out for myself the links between them. Occasionally I found myself objecting to some of the metaphysical conceits into which, along with his amazing mastery of English, Heschel sometimes falls: a worm on the island of Bikini Atoll shaking its fists at the atomic bomb (I prefer Emily Dickinson's image of a bird stamping its foot in the air) or, in imitation of Shakespeare, "We are such stuff as needs are made of, and our little life is rounded by a will."[1]

There is too a certain emotional insistence in Heschel's writings with which I have never been quite comfortable.

In trying to avoid the dangers of subjectivism, "pan-psychology," and ego-centeredness, Heschel frequently goes to the opposite extreme of treating meaning and value as "objective" realities outside of man to which man merely responds. To make this point even clearer, he speaks of God

1. Heschel, *Between God and Men*, 135.

as the subject and man as the object. "The structure which most characterizes Heschel's religious thought," writes Edward K. Kaplan, "is his *displacement of subjectivity*" from man to God."[2] This "subject–object" terminology appears incompatible with Heschel's dominant theme of genuinely reciprocal relationship between God and man. His assertion that the "I" is an "it" to God cannot be reconciled with his statement that God is compassionately concerned for the fate and the needs of every individual. If we are, in fact, embraced by the inner life of God, this does not mean that God thinks of humans as we think of an object, but rather that God relates to humans as persons in the truest sense of the term.

Heschel sets the human, or subjective, side of religion over against God's side; yet he also tells us that we do not know God in His essence but only what He demands of us, which means our relation with Him.

"Piety is a matter of life, not only a sense for the reality of the transcendent, but the taking of an adequate attitude toward it; not only a vision, a way to believe, but adjustment, the answer to a call, a mode of life."[3] The reality of piety that is set forth in this last statement is the reality of dialogue—not the nonreciprocal relation of a subject to an object but the reciprocal relation of an "I" to a "Thou."

We are, says Heschel, a "possession" of God, and our value resides not in ourselves but in what we stand for. Our essence does not possess the right to say "I," for what we call self is a monstrous deceit—something transcendent

2. See Kaplan, *Holiness in Words*, 173.

3. Heschel, *Man Is Not Alone*, 281.

in disguise. Will, freedom, life, and consciousness are im-
posed on us. "What is an 'I' to our minds is an 'It' to God."[4]
Heschel speaks of the presence of God as within man as
well as beyond him. But unless man's self can in some real
way be identified with this inner presence, the communion
of "the ineffable within" with "the ineffable beyond" cannot
be a real meeting of God and man. A genuinely reciprocal
relationship demands that man regard himself neither as
God's "possession" nor as an "object" of His thought, but as
a really free and responsible person—a partner in dialogue.

It was Heschel's feeling that I take his subject–object
dichotomy too seriously. "It is not the heart of the matter," he
said to me. In his formative years as a student he was, to be
sure, confronted by tendencies toward pan-psychologism,
relativism, and reduction to the sociological that he felt it
important to fight. But he did so not from the standpoint
of the older subject–object epistemology but from that of
phenomenology. "I use the phenomenological method to
analyze my own consciousness and that of those I respect,"
he said to me. "I use my own consciousness as a standard."
In this respect Heschel is close to Edmund Husserl—not
that he ever falls into Husserl's danger of solipsism, but in
that he tries to understand reality through analyzing the
structures of consciousness.

In contrast to Husserl's "transcendental ego," however,
Heschel stresses the exactly opposite perspective—knowing myself as known by the other rather than knowing the
other as known by myself. "Without knowing that when I
am before God I am nothing," Heschel said to me, "I have

4. Ibid., 126.

no position at all." It is in this sense that Heschel says, "I am an 'It' to God." "Only after Abraham realized he was dust and ashes could he argue with God." This is not the same as the Hasidic master Rabbi Bunam's saying that everyone must have two pockets to use as the occasion demands—in one of which is written, "For my sake the world was created," and in the other, "I am earth and ashes." For Heschel, as for Abraham, the "earth and ashes" definitely came first. "I do not really mean," Heschel explained to me, "that we have no right to say 'I.' But we have the right to say I only when we understand that the I is transcendence in disguise." When we deal with the mystery of self-consciousness, we must recognize that instead of self-consciousness lending meaning to consciousness, as Husserl held, it is itself in need of transcendent meaning. "To say that the I is an 'It' to God does not mean that God regards us as an It. The I is an 'It' in the light of *our* awareness of God."

Therefore, Heschel felt that my objection applied to what he *said* but not to what he *meant*. Heschel was so God-intoxicated and aware of the eternal that, to him, the "I" was indeed an "It." Heschel felt that the concept of the "subjectivity of God" enabled him to combine two important ideas—the absolute transcendence of God *and* the idea of the "divine pathos," God's sharing in the suffering and history of man.

❊

The real essence of what Heschel is saying here, as elsewhere, is that "to be is to stand for."[5] Taken positively, this

5. Heschel, *God in Search of Man*, 413.

is a statement that many are willing to accept as a faithful and creative expression of the relation of man to God. God is not a means to our ends, and our value does not reside in ourselves alone. We are the creatures of a Creator who creates the world anew at every moment. We live by His grace, and even our freedom is sustained in that grace. We discover God's presence through the ineffable that we encounter in all things, and in our response to the ineffable we know ourselves as known by God. We find the meaning of our lives not in ourselves, therefore, but in our relation to what transcends us.

This also means, I hold, that our "being" is as real as our "standing for," that we are no mere instrument or tool of God. We become ourselves only through relation to what is more than ourselves. But it is only *through* our becoming ourselves, each of us in his or her own unique particularity and his or her own concrete situation, that our lives take on transcendent meaning.

9

God in Search of Man
A Philosophy of Judaism

"Indifference to the sublime wonder of living is the root of sin," writes Heschel.[1] Awe precedes faith and is the root of sin, for it is "an intuition for the creaturely dignity of all things and their preciousness to God."[2] Revelation, to Heschel, is human and divine at once. "Prophetic words are never detached from the concrete, historic situation." And the revelation is not of God's very self but of His relation to history. Revelation is a dialogue in which the prophet is an active partner, and the Bible is a record of both revelation and response. "More decisive than the origin of the Bible in God is the presence of God in the Bible," which we cannot sense except by our response to it. This also means the life of the people, uniquely committed through the Covenant to becoming a holy people. Man imitates God through walking in His ways of mercy and righteousness,

1. Heschel, *God in Search of Man*, 43.
2. Ibid., 75.

for the only image of God that we can make is our own life as an image of His will. Life consists of endless opportunities to sanctify the profane, to redeem the power of God from the chain of potentialities."[3]

Agreement of the heart with the spirit, not only the letter of law, is itself a requirement of the law. Above all, the Torah asks for love—love of God and love of neighbor—and all observance is training in the art of love. Ritual and *mitzvoth* must be carried out with both body and soul: "Thoughts, feelings, ensconced in the inwardness of man, deeds performed in the absence of the soul are incomplete."[4] Outward performance is but an aspect of the totality of a deed. "God asks for the heart," for *kavana*—that inner intention which redirects the whole person to God. But the way to *kavana* is through the deed. The meaning of the order of Jewish living can be comprehended only in prayer and response. "All *mitzvoth* are means of evoking in us awareness of living in the neighborhood of God, of living in the holy dimension."[5] Here is the practical, if not the philosophical link between Heschel's general philosophy of religion, which stresses the awareness of the ineffable, and his specific philosophy of Judaism.

I did not discover an adequate philosophical link in my reading of Heschel's works, and I told him this on many occasions. In what was perhaps our last conversation, Heschel wisely pointed out that one cannot rationalize or universalize a specific way of life, such as Judaism. It strikes me now, as I write, that it would be like having to

3. Ibid., 250.

4. Ibid., 307.

5. Heschel, *Between God and Man*, 184.

68

give a general philosophical explanation of the commitment that one makes when one marries one person rather than another! Only Heschel does not content himself with a general philosophy of religion but also offers a philosophy of Judaism, with many specific and helpful insights, to be sure, such as the "leap of action" and the "holy dimension" of Jewish deeds.

The Christian dichotomy of faith and works has never been an important problem for Judaism, writes Heschel; for Judaism is concerned with right living in which deed and thought are bound into one. Religion or ethics comes to grief when it emphasizes motive alone and stresses purity of heart to the exclusion of the purpose and substance of the good action. "What man does in his concrete, physical existence is directly relevant to the divine."[6]

Heschel frequently falls into a tendency to identify his categories and symbols of the ineffable with the ineffable itself, as I also pointed out to him. "The categories of religious thinking . . . are unique," he writes, and "on a level that is . . . immediate, ineffable, metasymbolic."[7] But "categories of religious thinking" are already, as such, a step beyond the "awareness of something that can be neither conceptualized nor symbolized."[8] "Religious thinking is in perpetual danger of giving primacy to concepts and dogmas and to forfeit the immediacy of insights," Heschel writes.[9] Yet "insights" are not themselves immediate, even if they are derived more directly from the awareness of

6. Heschel, *Moral Grandeur and Spritual Audacity*, 141.

7. Heschel, *God in Search of Man*, 103.

8. Ibid., 108.

9. Ibid., 116.

the ineffable than concepts. The fact that he is referring to a metasymbolic reality leads Heschel, like the modern Vedantists, to regard the images that he uses to point toward that reality as themselves beyond the symbolic. He overlooks the possibility that here, too, may exist that "profound disparity between experience and expression" of which he is so acutely aware in connection with concepts.

This may account in part for what will seem to some readers to be an unprepared transition from the sense of the ineffable to an acceptance of the unique authority of the Bible and the sacredness of Jewish law in which Heschel identifies the voice of God with objective tradition. Heschel does not, in my judgment, show sufficient recognition of the tension that may arise in the relationship of the sense of the ineffable to the inherited form. "The claim of Israel must be recognized *before* attempting an interpretation," he writes,[10] ignoring the fact that our acceptance of this claim already necessarily involves an interpretation.

Heschel tends, moreover, to divide revelation and observance into an objective form supplied by the tradition and a subjective spiritual content supplied by our inner response. God "gave us the text and we refine and complete it," Heschel writes.[11] "The word is but a clue; the real burden of understanding is upon the mind and soul of the reader."[12] The reasons Heschel gives for accepting the traditional form tend to fit into this same objective–subjective dichotomy: sometimes it is because it is the will of

10. Ibid., 420.

11. Ibid., 274.

12. Ibid., 183.

God and sometimes because through the order of Jewish living one can sense the presence of God.

Finally, aside from repeated assertion, Heschel gives no real answer to the question he himself raises of how we know that what is subjectively true—the sense of the ineffable—is transubjectively real, that is, genuinely alludes to or derives from the transcendent. "The indication of what transcends all things is given to us with the same immediacy as the things themselves," he writes in a central statement in *Man Is Not Alone*.[13] But in *God in Search of Man* he recognizes that the *assertion* that God is real transcends our pre-conceptual awareness of the ineffable. In his attempt to answer this question he speaks of our belief in God's reality as an "ontological presupposition" that questions the self and goes beyond self-consciousness.[14] But this ontological presupposition seems to be only another name for the awareness of the ineffable itself. Heschel later states that the "standard by which to test the veracity of religious insights" must be an idea, not an event, "a supreme idea in human thinking, a universal idea," and offers as this standard the idea of "*oneness or love*."[15]

However, in the chapter "One God" in *Man Not Alone* to which he refers us, Heschel shows that what he really means is no mere conception. He rejects oneness as an abstract, universal idea in favor of the understanding of God as "*togetherness of all beings in holy otherness*."[16] Such "togetherness" can perhaps be verified *in the life* of a

13. Heschel, *Man Is Not Alone*, 63.

14. Heschel, *God in Search of Man*, 114–24

15. Ibid., 161.

16. Heschel, *Man Is Not Alone*, 109.

person and in his or her relations to others, but it cannot be abstracted into a universal standard or test by which *objectively* to verify one's religious insights.

Both the moment of insight, which is the power of religious truth, as Heschel writes, and the oneness of love, which is its content, "may be conveyed by the one word: *transcendence*."[17] But this would seem to beg the question. How do we know that our insight is the product of the impact of transcendence, that its love is not a subjective emotion, its "oneness" not an abstract idea?

The answer that Heschel offers to this central question he himself raises seems to be either an abstract universality that contradicts his emphasis on events and immediacy or a reassertion that carries no added knowledge value. This in no way invalidates his basic religious insight that transcendent meaning is immediately given to us in our meeting with existence. But it does raise a question as to how fully he has succeeded in converting this insight into a consistent philosophy of religion.

Although Heschel accepted my criticism as a "challenge to bring out more clearly" the link between his general philosophy of religion and his philosophy of Judaism, he held that he had provided such a link in the philosophy of time expounded in his book *The Sabbath*. Nor did he think it necessary to offer more than a link. "Once I say to you I preserve my sense of mystery by putting on *tefillin* every day," he said to me, "I do not need to say, 'Why *tefillin*?'" There must be room for "historical contingencies." There is, indeed, no way to remain in the "universal" and

17. Heschel, *God in Search of Man*, 162.

ground *any* particular religious tradition or practice on it. That is, no particular religion can ever be justified in the general. This would be to reduce philosophy of religion to an affair of Platonic ideas above concrete space and time.

Perhaps a similar objection applies to my question as to how we know that what is subjectively true is transsubjectively real. Heschel himself said to me that there is no answer to that question; for "you cannot epistemologically and logically demonstrate the transcendent by immanent means." The important link for Heschel is that the "ineffable beyond" is known *with the same immediacy* as the "ineffable within."

The great contribution of *God in Search of Man*, in my opinion, is that it presents the heart of Judaism in unusually broad, rich, and intensive scope. This book is of profound significance to Christianity, both as an interpretation of biblical categories and as a correction of common misconceptions of traditional Judaism as stressing a legalistic observance of externals. At the same time, it strikes a powerful blow against the "religious behaviorism" of many liberal and Reconstructionist Jews that maintains the inherited customs and rituals of Judaism merely out of respect for tradition or a desire to perpetuate "Jewish civilization." Most important of all, it offers a positive interpretation and understanding of Judaism capable of evoking the highest devotion. "Bringing to light the lonely splendor of Jewish thinking, conveying the taste of eternity in our daily living is the greatest aid we can render to the man of our time who has fallen so low that he is not even capable of being ashamed of what has happened in his days."[18]

18. Ibid., 421.

The primary difficulty of the modern Jew, Heschel rightly observes, is not his inability to comprehend the *divine origin* of the law, but his inability to sense the presence of divine meaning in the fulfillment of the law. But the modern Jew's sense of the ineffable does not necessarily lead him to follow Heschel in accepting the prescriptions of the law as an objective order of divine will.

The presence of divine meaning in the observance of the law comes to us through our very commitment to and participation in that observance, writes Heschel. But if those who are not observant Jews do not *now* feel themselves commanded by God to perform the law, how can they perform it with integrity even on the strength of Heschel's assurance that they *shall* know this to be God's will for them through their observance?

"Heschel does not require the transition from the sense of the ineffable to Torah and *mitzvoth*," writes Professor Lou H. Silberman in reply to my criticism above. "Indeed, . . . these three are one; hence each must be made available, for all are ultimately required."[19] To say this is to miss the central problem in Heschel's philosophy: the transition from his general philosophy of religion to his specific philosophy of Judaism.

We can certainly agree with Professor Silberman, however, when he adds, "The real problem is not that one is more available, but that all three are all but unavailable to the contemporary Jew."[20] Heschel's concern is to make us aware of the possibility of sensing the ineffable in the world, in Torah, in *mitzvoth*.

19. Silberman, "The Philosophy of Abraham Heschel," 26.
20. Ibid.

For those outside these three, Heschel's thought is and will increasingly be one of the richest sources for confrontation both with modern religious thought and with the whole range of the Jewish tradition.

Part Four

Prophecy, Social Action,
and Existentialism

10

The Prophets
Divine Pathos

Although *The Prophets* is a continuation of Heschel's religious philosophy as it was developed in *Man Is Not Alone* and *God in Search of Man,* its original core was a slim German volume *Die Prophetie,* Heschel's doctoral dissertation published in German in Poland in 1936. This earlier work was the germ of some of Heschel's seminal ideas—the prophets' sympathy with the divine pathos, man knowing himself as known by God, the emphasis on the relationship between man and God as opposed to the Greek description of God's nature and attributes. This original core is expanded in *The Prophets* into a "theology of pathos," which is one of the most significant original contributions to biblical thought in our time.

The person who immerses himself in the prophets' words "exposes himself to a ceaseless shattering of indifference, and one needs a skull of stone to remain callous to such blows."[1] This is because the prophets' words are

1. Heschel, *The Prophets,* xii.

onslaughts that shatter false security rather than general ideas about which one may reflect. Responding to Martin Heidegger's astonishingly naïve and uniformed statement that the prophets of Israel announce "the God upon whom the certainty of salvation in a supernatural blessedness reckons," Martin Buber wrote that the prophets of Israel "have always wished to shatter all security and to proclaim in the opened abyss of the final insecurity the unwished-for God who demands that His human creatures become real, that they become human, and confounds all who imagine that they can take refuge in the certainty that the temple of God is in their midst."[2] It would be salutary if the contemporary fundamentalists among both Christians and Jews would take heed to these words!

Another way of knowing opens up to us in communion with the prophets, writes Heschel: our surrender to their impact leads to "moments in which the mind peals off, as it were, its not-knowing" and comprehends by being comprehended.[3] The prophet does not deal, like modern man, with meaninglessnesss but with deafness to meaning, and the meaning that he speaks is not one of timeless ideas but of the divine understanding of a human situation. Heschel defines prophecy, in fact, as "an exegesis of existence from a divine perspective," and he places this exegesis squarely before us as an answer to our despair: "it is for us to decide whether freedom is self-assertion or response to a demand, whether the ultimate situation is conflict or concern."[4]

2. Quoted in Friedman, *Martin Buber's Life and Work*, 2:165.

3. Heschel, *The Prophets*, 1:xxvi–xxvii.

4. Ibid., xiv–xv.

The prophet discloses a *divine pathos*, not just a divine judgment. This means, to Heschel, that God is involved with man, bound through a personal relationship to Israel, and that the prophet is a partner and associate rather than a mouthpiece or an instrument of God. This approach leads Heschel to speak of God's inner life—the "dramatic tension in God" between His anger and His compassion— and of God's heart, which the prophet feels. Whereas Martin Buber sees Hosea's marriage to a prostitute as a living symbol of Israel that has betrayed God, Heschel sees it as the education of Hosea himself in the understanding of divine sensibility. The prophet has sympathy at the same time for both God and the people. "Speaking to the people he is emotionally at one with God; in the presence of God . . . he is emotionally at one with the people."[5]

In *The Prophets* Heschel's writing takes on a greater moral force than ever before. "The prophets were the first men in history to regard a nation's reliance upon force as evil," he writes.[6] They discover that history is a nightmare full of a corruption that we dare not accept as God's creation. (Although their approaches to history are radically different, the historian of religion Mircea Eliade uses these identical words to describe history.) "Others may be satisfied with improvement," Heschel writes, "the prophets demand redemption."[7] God's demand for justice means not only outward duty but the love of the heart. Knowledge of God does not turn man away from man. It means sharing God's concern for justice, sympathy in action. Injustice is

5. Ibid., 87.
6. Ibid., 212.
7. Ibid., 231.

condemned not because a law if broken but because a person is hurt, a person whose anguish may reach the heart of God. The prophets do not discuss ideas and norms, like the moralists. They demand and insist that what ought to be shall be. "In the eyes of the prophets justice . . . is charged with the omnipotence of God."[8]

Heschel's theology of pathos is formed in conscious contrast to the Stoic doctrine of the divine *apatheia*, as well as to the classical theology that discusses the nature and attributes of God as He is in Himself. Like Martin Heidegger, Heschel recognizes that we cannot take being for granted, but unlike him he stresses that being is not *all*. Biblical man begins not with being but with the surprise of being and cannot identify being, even as the source of all things, with ultimate reality. Neither can he consider the Being that calls a reality into existence as of the same nature as being itself. On the contrary, it "transcends mysteriously all conceivable being." "Creation is a mystery; being as being is an abstraction." This contrast between Creation and being illuminates the unbiblical nature of that Heideggerian ontology that has been taken over by such modern theologians as Paul Tillich and Rudolf Bultmann.

Heschel has shown the impossibility of separating God's being from his doing and has pointed to "anthropopathy" as "a genuine insight into God's relatedness to man rather than a projection of human traits into divinity."[9] Expressions of pathos may help evoke our sense of God's realness and aliveness if we take them as allusions rather

8. Ibid., 272.
9. Quoted in Kaplan, *Holiness in Words*, 57.

than descriptions, understatements rather than adequate accounts.

It is difficult nonetheless for us to understand pathos as a transitive interpersonal reality rather than an internal, psychological one. This is particularly so because of the opposition Heschel sets up between the apathy of the Stoic God and the pathos of the biblical God. We cannot help but remove pathos into the inner life of God as Heschel does himself at times. The dialogue between God and man is not within God, of course, and the communication of God's mercy and anger is an essential part of that dialogue. Yet when we talk of God's pathos and the prophet's sympathy with it, it is difficult not to attribute feelings to God very like those of ours, even if infinitely greater than ours. Thus Heschel cannot altogether escape the problem of anthropomorphism, nor does he wish to. "Anthropomorphic language may be preferable to abstract language," Heschel said to me, "for when you use abstract language, you may have the illusion of adequacy."

The most trenchant application that Heschel makes of his theology of pathos is his treatment of the meaning and mystery of God's wrath. In our culture there are still a great many who persist in setting an "Old Testament God of wrath" in opposition to a "New Testament God of love." Heschel, in contrast, points out that God's anger and His love are not opposites but correlatives. God's anger is *suspended* love, mercy withheld or concealed for the sake of love in order that compassion may resume. In contradistinction to Rudolf Otto, who sees God's love as "nothing but quenched wrath" and who sees wrath itself as arbitrary and irrational, Heschel insists that the normal and original pathos is love or mercy and that God's anger is a moral judgment preceded and followed by compassion.

The Stoic sage is homo *apatheitkos*; the prophet, to Heschel, is homo *sympathetikos*. Sympathy has a dialogical structure, says Heschel. It is open to the presence of another person and to his feeling. It is not an end in itself, like ecstasy, but leads to action. "It is not a goal but a sense of challenge, a commitment, a state of tension, consternation, and dismay."[10] In this it is related to Heschel's "awareness of the ineffable," which becomes religion only when it is experienced as a question to which our lives must be the answer. The prophetic sympathy is not spontaneous but is a response to God's pathos that comes of being attuned to Him. This attunement is more than a feeling; it is a whole way of being. "In contrast to ecstasy, with its momentary transports, sympathy with God is a constant attitude." When the prophet gives the message of God's anger, he is concerned not only about the punishment that may descend upon the people but also about the disturbance of God that only man's contrition, shame, and repentance can assuage. Sympathy, used here for the first time as a theological category, is not to be understood cosmologically but anthropologically as man's immediate relation to the divine pathos. "It is as nonbiblical to separate emotion or passion from spirit as it is to disparage emotion or passion . . . Emotion is a state of being filled with the spirit which is above all a state of being moved."[11]

Heschel contrasts the union with God in mystic ecstasy with the prophet's dialogue with God. "The prophet

10. Heschel, *The Prophets*, 2:88–89.

11. Ibid., 405.

is responsive not only receptive";[12] his personality is not dissolved but intensely present and fervently involved; he is fully conscious of the present and the past; he is not ravished by delight but receives the revelation against his will; he does not have an experience but a task. Prophecy is meeting between God and man without fusion. The dialogical structure, which is never fully clear when Heschel discusses divine pathos in itself, becomes unmistakable here. The prophet's "response to what is disclosed to him turns revelation into dialogue";[13] the prophetic person stands over against the divine person in a "subject–subject relationship." "The prophet encounters real otherness, else there would be no mission, but also retains the fullness of his own person, else there would be no vocation." The prophet encounters not a timeless idea but an act of giving a word and a pathos in time, springing from a divine Presence "who becomes involved and engaged in the encounter with man." God does not reveal himself, nor does the prophet speak of God as He is in Himself, as ultimate being. "It is God in relation to humanity, to the world Who is the theme of his words." Prophecy is "anthropotropic" rather than "theotropic"; it directs the prophet to man not to God and thus assures the divine concern for man's moral life in the here and now.

For all this emphasis upon the dialogic relationship between God and man in prophecy, Heschel never attains decisive clarity on this subject. One reason for this is the ambiguity of the word "pathos," which cannot altogether be divorced from an inner state or feeling. Thus Heschel

12. Ibid., 137.

13. Heschel, *God in Search of Man*, 260.

describes prophetic inspiration as "an event in the life of God" that "happens in God in relation to the prophet."[14] Another reason for this unclarity is Heschel's desire to show man's relationship to God as the opposite of the ordinary subject–object relation. In clear contradistinction to his repeated emphasis on the prophet's relationship with God as a subject–subject one, he speaks in his "Conclusions" of man as "being an object of the divine Subject." "For prophetic apprehension, God is never an 'it' but is constantly given as a personal spirit, manifesting Himself as subject even in the act of thought addressed to Him." God is encountered "not as universal, general pure Being but always . . . as a specific pathos that comes with a demand in a concrete situation." All we know of God is His knowledge of and concern for us; we discover "ourselves as the object of His thinking."

If Heschel were to use the language of I and Thou, he would speak, like the Protestant theologian Emil Brunner, of a "Thou-I" relationship in which the initiative is entirely on the side of God. "In view of the gulf which yawns between divine infinitude and the limitations of the human situation," writes Heschel, a divine–human understanding is ultimately contingent upon divine anticipation and expectation." In his concluding section, "The Dialectic of the Divine–Human Encounter," Heschel describes the "twofold mutual initiative" as one in which "the subject—man—becomes object and the object—God—becomes subject."

14. Ibid., 198–99.

This problem is not merely one of inconsistent terminology. There seems to be a still unworked-through unclarity in the relation between Heschel's divine pathos, in which "the primary factor is our being seen and known by Him," and the dialogical structure of the prophetic relationship that he stresses in *God in Search of Man* and *The Prophets*.

To raise one more problem, in *God in Search of Man* Heschel says that what is important is not our certainty of the origin of the Bible in God but our awareness of the presence of God in the Bible. In *The Prophets*, however, he says that the validity and distinction of the prophetic message lies in its origin in God. The prophet's "certainty of being inspired by God," writes Heschel, is based on "the source of his experience" in God. Having an experience is indeed not central to the prophet, but neither can his "certainty" of the source be objectified into an independent knowledge apart from his relationship with God.

Heschel does not actually wish to see this certainty objectified in this way. The unshakable conviction of Jeremiah and Amos that they speak for God might be better understood, in my opinion, in terms of God's call and the prophet's response than in terms of any certainty or even emotional oneness with God that might seem to put the prophet on God's side of the divine–human meeting. Heschel himself said to me that he has pointed to the centrality of the prophet's certainty of being inspired by God not as a dogma but in the sense of Jeremiah's "Of a truth the Lord has sent me," hence as a consciousness of a call.

11

The Insecurity of Freedom
Heschel's Social Action

It is no coincidence, as Franklin Sherman has pointed out, that the resumption of Heschel's work on the prophets and the publication of his 1962 book *The Prophets* "corresponded in time with his own emergence as a spokesman on social issues of the day." If "situational thinking" and "depth theology," as Heschel defines them, are an endeavor to rediscover the questions to which religion is an answer, they must also include the authentification of one's truth in one's concrete existence. The most heartening aspect of Heschel's activity is that he did not confine it to an abstract mysticism or interpretation of Jewish thought but, again and again in the last years of his life, verified his truths by being true to them himself: in the march at Selma, Alabama; in picketing the Soviet legation because of the treatment of Soviet Jews; in co-chairing the national committee of Clergy and Laymen against the War in Vietnam; in speaking and acting for Israel in the time of its danger;

in social protest and concern about medicine, old age, race relations. His book *The Insecurity of Freedom* stands as a great living witness to all these concerns.

One of the most frequently repeated motifs of Heschel's social witness was his condemnation of the central emphasis in American culture on success and power. "More people die of success than cancer," Heschel dared to tell the members of the American Medical Association. And to a White House Conference on children and youth he declared that we are threatened by degradation through power: knowledge as success, values justified solely in terms of expediency, an instrumentalization of the world that leads to the instrumentalization of man. "The evil, the falsehood, the vulgarity of our way of living cry to high heaven," writes Heschel in *The Insecurity of Freedom*.[1] Our age, says Heschel, is the "age of suspicion," and its Golden Rule is "Suspect thy neighbor as thyself."[2] The corruption of values, moreover, means a corruption of the word: "Words have become pretexts in the technique of evading the necessity of honest and genuine expression."[3]

Our culture cannot be redeemed of its vulgarity through teaching moral *values*, but only through character education, *cultivation of total sensitivity*. The antecedents to moral commitment are acts and moments within the depth. "You can affect a person only if you reach his inner life, the level where every human being is insecure and feels his incompleteness, the level of awareness that lies beyond

1. Heschel, *The Insecurity of Freedom*, 218.

2. Ibid., 17.

3. Ibid.

articulation."[4] One discovers his soul not through turning inward, however, but through transcending one's self in response to the call of ends that surpass one's interest and needs. This sort of character education is not a mere means to the end of training or success. It is an intrinsic value. In a paper presented at a White House Conference on Aging, Heschel proposed "senior universities" where the purpose of learning is not a career but learning itself.

Heschel's social witness expressed itself positively in his co-chairmanship of Clergy and Laymen Against the War in Vietnam, of which he was the founder. He was a tireless fighter against the United States' engagement in Indochina. In Heschel's paper to the White House Conference on Children and Youth, his witness for social justice also rang out loud and clear: the protest against this country's squandering of material resources on luxuries when more than a billion people go to bed hungry every night, his protest against our treatment of the black people of America. In the opening address at the National Conference on Religion and Race in Chicago in 1963, Heschel struck out with all possible force against racism—that unmitigated evil which is man's gravest threat, combining, as it does, the maximum of cruelty and the minimum of thought. "What begins as inequality of some inevitably ends as inequality of all."[5] Even the wholeness of the religious man is eaten away by the cancer of racism: "Prayer and prejudice cannot dwell in the same heart. Worship without compassion is . . . an abomination."[6]

4. Ibid., 58.
5. Ibid., 87.
6. Ibid.

Heschel's constant motif of embarrassment before God now becomes embarrassment before the black man, on whom his very presence inflicts insult. "I, the white man, have become in the eyes of others a symbol of arrogance and pretension, giving offense to other human beings, hurting their pride, even without intending it."[7]

Unlike the New Leftists, Heschel could not combine concern for the plight of the black man with indifference to the fate of the Jews in Soviet Russia. "Discrimination against the political rights of the Negro in America and discrimination against the religious and cultural rights of the Jews in the Soviet Union are indivisible."[8] What is today a widespread movement of protest, Heschel began as an almost single-handed fight. It is he who made his younger friend, the novelist Elie Wiesel, aware of the situation of the Russian Jews and prompted Wiesel to go to Moscow and to write *The Jews of Silence*. Like Elie Wiesel, Heschel speaks of the moral trauma that haunts the Jews in free countries for failing to do their utmost to save the Jews under Hitler and the nightmare possibility of a new tragic dereliction of duty. Spiritual slavery makes impossible personal wholeness and intellectual creativity for the Russian Jew. What Heschel pleads for is not special privilege but equality—the rights, guaranteed the Russian Jews by the Soviet constitution but systematically refused them in practice: to teach, to hear, to read literature, to communicate with those with a common spiritual heritage. As with the black man in America, "Discrimination against the religious and cultural rights of the Jews in the Soviet Union

7. Ibid., 88.

8. Heschel, *Moral Grandeur and Spiritual Audacity*, 214.

is a disease that sooner or later will affect the human situation everywhere."[9] It is we, says Heschel, who must speak for the "Jews of silence"; they have no voice. "We must cry in public because they can only cry in secrecy."[10]

We cannot fail to mention the major role Heschel played in the work of Cardinal Bea at the Second Vatican Council to secure a statement on the Jews that would help to end two millennia of built-in Christian anti-Semitism, including a secret personal visit that Heschel paid at that time to the Pope at the latter's request. Later the Pope himself played a significant part in the publication and distribution of Heschel's works in Italy. The letter that Heschel wrote at the time, that he saw the Second Vatican Council as falling back into Christian triumphalism, bears witness to his passionate concern.

Heschel's great concern as to the outcome of the council's statement on the Jews in letters and in other ways has been well documented. The leading public Quaker, Douglas Steere, who was the representative of the Society of Friends to the Second Vatican Counsel, told me of the frequent calls that Heschel would make to Steere from Rome. "Douglas," said Steere to me, imitating Heschel's accent, "we must do something about this!"

In his letter of September 3, 1964, Heschel wrote in part:

> A message that regards the Jew as a candidate for conversion and proclaims that it is the fate of Judaism to disappear will be abhorred by Jews all over the world and is bound to foster bitterness and resentment.

9. Heschel, *The Insecurity of Freedom*, 283.
10. Ibid.

As I have repeatedly stated to leading personalities of the Vatican, I am ready to go to Auschwitz any time if faced with the alternative of conversion or death.

Jews throughout the world will be dismayed by a call from the Vatican to abandon their faith in a generation that witnessed the massacre of six millions Jews and the destruction of thousands of synagogues on a continent where the dominant religion was not Islam, Buddhism, or Shintoism.[11]

In a letter to *The New York Times* before the presidential election of 1972, Heschel warned of the corruption that had penetrated to the highest places in our government, and he asked how Amos, Isaiah, and Jeremiah would have responded to our situation. Heschel tried unsuccessfully at that time to convince his co-leaders in Clergy and Laymen against the War in Vietnam to call for an independent body that might act as the "conscience" for the government. In the light of the events of the months following Heschel's death in December 1972, culminating in Nixon's resignation, these actions appear strikingly prophetic in the popular sense of the term as well as in the sense of the prophetic demand for justice.

All these were *not* the passing foibles of a great spiritual leader who had fallen victim to the "styles and fads" of the 1960s, as Heschel's former student and disciple, Professor Jacob Neusner, suggested in a memorial issue of the Catholic journal *America* devoted to Heschel. On the contrary, they were the unmistakable carrying over of the indignation and compassion of the biblical prophets to the concrete social existence of our time.

11. Quoted from Tannenbaum, "Jewish-Christian Relations," 309.

12

Who Is Man?

Existentialism of Dialogue

The title of Heschel's book *Who Is Man?* implies that man cannot be understood from the outside as an object of impartial investigation, but only from within as the fruit of self-understanding. This title links our understanding of our own uniqueness and our understanding of human being. A more felicitous way of pointlng to this link, as I have suggested in my book *To Deny Our Nothingness*, is to speak of the "image of man," or "the image of the human." Heschel does, in fact, speak of the image of man in just this way: "The decisions, norms, preferences affecting both action and motivation are not simply part of human nature; they are determined by the image of man we are committed to, by the ultimate context to which we seek to relate ourselves."[1]

We are not simply defined as human from without. We become human through making decisions, through

1. Heschel, *Who Is Man?*, 8.

discovering "the value involved in human being," through confronting the conflict between existence and expectation that makes our self a problem to ourselves.

Man has always been a problem to himself, as the Book of Job and the Psalms amply testify. But in our age the terrifying seriousness of the human situation has come into focus in a way that would have been unthinkable before Auschwitz. Stripped of our assumptions and illusions, we cannot "think about the human situation without shame, anguish, and disgust." The note of embarrassment at being human that is so often present in Heschel's writings becomes most pronounced in *Who Is Man?* Like a latter-day Pascal, Heschel uncovers behind man's self-satisfaction a poor, needy, vulnerable creature, "always on the verge of misery." "Scratch his skin and you come upon bereavement, affliction, uncertainty, fear, and pain."

The skepticism of contemporary man is not about God but about man. "Today it is the humanity of man that is no longer self-evident." How can a human being achieve certainty of his humanity in the face of the massive defamation of man that led and may lead again to physical extermination? If we explain man as a thing, we miss the mystery and surprise that constitute his existence as a person. Man "is a being who asks questions concerning himself," and his first question is how to turn his "human being" into "being human," how to become really human.

It is not morality in the sense of some external moral act that is the problem but the self itself: our life itself is the task, problem, and challenge. We do not begin with an abstract moral 'ought' but with the love of being alive and the claim that this love places on us. Our task is to respond to the call that addresses us as persons in order to become more than we are. Like Albert Camus, Heschel sees man as both "solitary" and "solidary." We understand man through understanding our selves, but we do not rest in subjectivity. To be man means to be with other human beings. Human existence is coexistence, sharing, solidarity. "*The dignity of human existence is in the power of reciprocity*," and this reciprocity extends even to man's most personal concern, his search for meaning.[2] Not only social living but the humanities are rooted in man's care for man. "The degree to which one is sensitive to other people's suffering, to other men's humanity, is the index of one's own humanity."[3] This does not in the least imply that for Heschel the self is purely social. "Life comprises not only arable, productive land, but also mountains of dreams, an underground of sorrow, towers of yearning, which can hardly be utilized to the last for the good of society."[4]

Unlike Paul Tillich, Heschel does not see the main threat to man as the fear of nonbeing but the fear of *meaningless* being. Unlike Martin Heidegger, he does not stop with the mystery of being but goes beyond it to the mystery of man. "Man is a fountain of immense meaning, not a drop in the ocean of being."[5]

2. Ibid., 46.

3. Ibid.

4. Ibid., 59.

5. Heschel, *Man Is Not Alone*, 208.

Heschel's divergence from such thinkers as Heidegger and Tillich does not mean that he is less existentialist than they. "Ideas, formulas, or doctrines are generalities, impersonal, timeless," writes Heschel, "and as such they remain incongruous with the essential mode of human existence which is concrete, personal, here and now."[6] The infinite meaning to which all things allude is not an *object*, a self-subsistent, timeless idea or value—but *a presence*. To Heschel transcendence is not an article of faith but "what we come upon immediately when standing face to face with reality." An ultimate being that is not related to us and does not care about us can be of no concern to us.

Living, to Heschel, means lending form to sheer being. Heidegger and Tillich to the contrary, our central fear is not the fear of death but of life "branded with the unerasable shock at absurdity, cruelty, and callousness."[7] The primary problem is how to shape our total existence as a pattern of meaning. "Right living is like a work of art, the product of a vision and of a wrestling with concrete situations."[8]

There is a new note of absurdity in *Who Is Man?* that brings Heschel surprisingly close to Camus. The vocation of man, Heschel suggests, may be "to live in defiance of absurdity, notwithstanding futility and defeat; to attain faith in God even in spite of God."[9] Nonetheless, in contrast to Camus, Heschel holds that the supreme philosophical question is not suicide but martyrdom: What is worth

6. Heschel, *Who Is Man?*, 79.

7. Ibid., 96.

8. Ibid., 99.

9. Ibid., 80.

dying for? If Heschel follows Nietzsche in his image of man as a short, critical stage between the animal and the spiritual, he advances the Jewish *kiddush ha-shem*—the readiness to die for the sake of God—in explicit contrast to Nietzsche's *amor fati,* or acceptance of fate. To be ready to die for God's name also means to sanctify God's name in one's living. "We are constantly in the mills of death, but we are also the contemporaries of God."[10] Heschel's ultimate emphasis is not upon absurdity or death but upon our built-in awareness "of being *called* upon . . . to live in a way which is compatible with the grandeur and mystery of living."[11]

Heschel saw death as an integral part of his existentialism of dialogue, of the partnership between God and man. In a series of reflections on death that Heschel delivered at an international congress on death in 1969, Heschel rejected the focus on the specifics of individual immortality in favor of trust in the relationship with God. "Eternity is not perpetual future but perpetual presence." Hence Heschel's emphasis is not on the "hereafter" but on the "herenow."

This is the meaning of death: the ultimate self-dedication to the divine. Death so understood will not be distorted by the craving for immortality, for this act of giving away is reciprocity on man's part for God's gift of life. "For the pious man it is a privilege to die."[12]

10. Ibid., 102.

11. Ibid., 110.

12. Heschel, *Moral Grandeur and Spiritual Audacity*, 317.

I have dealt with Heschel as a philosopher rather than as a theologian because he does have an original philosophy that, however unsystematic, includes all the aspects of a comprehensive philosophy: an ontology, a theory of knowledge, a theory of values, an ethics, a metaphysics, or a philosophy of religion, and applications in many concrete fields. Heschel is mainly interested in the philosophy of religion and theology, to be sure, but he recognizes that "the primary issue of theology is *pre-theological;* it is the total situation of man and his attitudes toward life and the world."[13] We may speak of Heschel as an existentialist (which is important to me at least since I am the author of what is still the definitive anthology of existentialist authors—*The Worlds of Existentialism: A Critical Reader*), on the basis of his contrast between the evocative, unique, insightful, responsive character of "depth theology" and the universal, abstract, declarative, creedal, and authoritarian nature of theology. Not that Heschel accepts the one and rejects the other. He insists, here as elsewhere, on the necessity of keeping alive the polarity of doctrine and insight, dogma and faith, ritual and response, institution and individual. "We sense the ineffable in one realm; we name and exploit reality in another. To maintain the right balance of mystery and meaning, of stillness and utterance, of reverence and action seems to be the goal of religious existence."[14]

13. Ibid., 296.

14. Heschel, *The Insecurity of Freedom*, 122.

Heschel recognizes, to be sure, that "without the spontaneity of the person, response and inner identification, without the sympathy of understanding, the body of tradition crumbles between the fingers."[15] But he does not adequately recognize the gap that remains between the two even when one holds on simultaneously to both the subjective and the objective, nor the possibility of another form of handing down, less explicit and systematic but more integral in its relation to the depth theology that gave rise to it.

Actually Heschel's writing itself points to this other possibility. He has not abstracted his insights into clear-cut formulae but has retained in his very style the traces of the reality to which he points. Poetry and philosophy, wonder and thought conjoined produce a philosophy that does not *define* but *points,* a theology that does not describe but evokes. At the heart of this philosophy lies a trust that informs human deeds rather than replaces them, that gives courage to live in insecurity rather than offers any sure groundwork of faith. "Trust in God *is* God," is God's presence, says Heschel in *Israel: An Echo of Eternity.* "The person in whom I trust is present in my trust . . . Waiting for Him becomes waiting with Him, sharing in the coming."[16]

This motif of trust, which Heschel himself does not single out as such, runs like a connecting link through all his philosophy and through the "ways of deeds" to which he points. In place of the dichotomy of outer deeds and inner intention, Heschel stresses trust: "We are not obliged

15. Ibid., 118.

16. Heschel, *Israel: An Echo of Eternity*, 96.

to be perfect once for all, but only to rise again and again."[17]
"Judaism insists upon the deed and hopes for the intention," writes Heschel.[18] More than that, the act, life itself, educates the will. One need not wait for the good motive before doing the good. It comes into being in the very act of doing. But this also means, to Heschel as to the prophets, that it is an act of evil to accept the state of evil as either inevitable or final, whether because of a view of human nature or of the world. The reality of God's love is greater than "the law of love." Where the latter places upon us an impossible demand, God accepts us in all our frailty and weakness. This means an active partnership of man and God, rather than despairing of sinful man and passively relying on the grace of God.

Heschel's understanding of prayer is, in his own special sense, that of dialogue: "The purpose of prayer is to be brought to God's attention: to be listened to, to be understood by Him."[19] This means that the gate to grace lies in our making our existence *worthy* of being known to God. For God to be present we have to be God's witnesses, and this means, even in prayer, that tension of trust and contending that was present in Abraham, Jacob, and Job, in the Baal Shem Tov and Levi Yitzhak of Berditchev, in Martin Buber, Abraham Joshua Heschel, and Elie Wiesel. We pray the way we live: "Ultimately, there is only one way of gaining certainty of the realness of any reality, and that is by knocking our heads against the wall. Then we discover there is something real outside the mind."

17. Heschel, *The Insecurity of Freedom*, 140.
18. Ibid.
19. Ibid., 256.

In a three-way correspondence between Martin Buber, the great Protestant theologian Reinhold Niebuhr, and myself, Buber used this same image to describe his approach to social problems: "I cannot know how much justice is possible in a given situation," Buber wrote, "unless I go on until my head hits the wall and hurts."[20] For Abraham Heschel, as for his and my friend Martin Buber, there is no essential difference between the life of prayer and the life of action. "A religious man," writes Heschel, "is a person who holds God and man in one thought at one time, at all times, who suffers in himself harms done to others, whose greatest passion is compassion, whose greatest strength is love and defiance of despair."[21] Heschel himself was that religious man.

---

20. Quoted in Friedman, *Martin Buber and the Social Sciences*, 15.
21. Heschel, *The Insecurity of Freedom*, 183.

Part Five

God Follows Me Everywhere

13

I Asked for Wonder
Heschel's Last Years

I was terribly shocked by the news of Heschel's heart attack that occurred two years before his death, and still
more by his thin and wan appearance when he returned to
New York. He told me in detail of the whole attack, clearly
as a warning, and made me promise to lose weight. He
had gone to Detroit for a lecture, could not find a taxi, and
ended up walking many blocks with two heavy suitcases.
He awoke at four in the morning with a severe heart attack.
In the course of receiving blood transfusions he contracted
hepatitis, so despite a year in Florida, he ended up looking
twenty to thirty years older than he had before. He told
me that when he lay in the intensive care unit in a hospital
in New York City and was visited by his younger friend
and disciple, Rabbi Wolfe Kelman, he exclaimed, "I, who
wrote a book entitled *Who Is Man?*, must now lie here like
a beast!"

A few years ago Rabbi Samuel H. Dresner brought out a beautiful spiritual anthology of Heschel's writings titled *I Asked for Wonder*. The photograph that he put on the front of his book was one taken after the ravages of heart attack and hepatitis. Although this was not in any way Dr. Dresner's meaning, I could not help feeling as if the photograph was a reproach, saying, "I asked for wonder, and this is what I got!" Perhaps because my face does not reflect either illness or great spiritual suffering, it is hard for me to take in that at the moment of writing I am eighteen years older than Heschel was when he died!

Perhaps Heschel was not a prophet without honor in his own country, but he lived and died the life of a prophet—God's witness and ours at the same time. When I told Heschel in our last face to face talk that I had decided to give up my position at Temple University for a more limited commitment at San Diego State University, he was genuinely delighted. "The center of America is moving to the West Coast," he said, "and in any case you will have more time to study and to write."

When I first visited Heschel at the seminary thirty years before this, he told me how his colleagues laughed at his concern for Jewish piety. By the end of his life Heschel had become a dominant force at the seminary and in America and world Judaism, as well as having a great impact on Catholic and Protestant thought. What particularly pleased me was the fact that Heschel was not afraid to risk himself through social witness. After years of concentrating on study and writing, producing one remarkable book after the other over the whole span of Jewish life and thought, Heschel emerged as one of the clearest and strongest voices in social action in America. He spoke tirelessly on behalf of the old, the sick, the discriminated against, and he marched with Martin Luther King Jr. in Selma. He gave me with pride an article transcribing "A Conversation with Martin Luther King" at the Rabbinical Assembly ten days before King was assassinated, in which Heschel introduced King. King spoke of Heschel as "one of the truly great men of our day and age," a "truly great prophet," "relevant at all times."

The easier life that Heschel urged on me, he was incapable of leading himself. He looked so full of his old vitality and spirit when I saw him in early November 1972 that I was totally unprepared for the news of his death in late December. *Newsweek*'s sympathetic account of his last week of life showed me how far he was from being able to give up himself the stimulation of the East Coast. How could he indeed—at the very height of his influence? My only comfort—a small but real one—regards Heschel's trip to Connecticut to greet Philip Berrigan on his release from Danbury Prison. David Lichtman, a young friend and former student of mine who had never met Heschel (and who is today, as a disciple of the Satmor rebbe, far more orthodox than Heschel himself was), drove Heschel home from Danbury Prison. David told me that on the way home a part of their conversation was their very different relationship to me. Thus I knew myself as in the mind of Heschel three days before he died—not without analogy to Heschel's own conception that we know ourselves as known by God!

I learned of Heschel's death indirectly and without any details. While I was still wondering whom to contact to find out about the funeral (I did not yet know how quickly Orthodox law demands that someone who has died be buried), Elie Wiesel called me and told me he had just come from the funeral. When I next visited Elie, he read me Heschel's early Yiddish poem that he had read at the funeral— a poem remarkably in the spirit of Elie himself:

GOD FOLLOWS ME EVERYWHERE

God follows me everywhere,
Weaving a web of visions around me,
Blinding my sightless spine like a sun.

God follows me like an enveloping forest
And continually astonishes my lips into awesome silence
Like a child lost in an ancient sanctuary.

God follows me within me like a mirror.
I want to rest. He demands. Come,
See how visions lie aimlessly scattered in the streets.

O wander, deep in my own fantasies, like a secret,
Down a long corridor through the world.
Now and then, high above me,
I catch a glimpse of the faceless face of God.[1]

Elie's reading this poem to me and my writing these reminiscences has helped me mourn a dear friend and a beloved teacher.

Thirteen years later I was much moved to learn of a meeting between Heschel and Wiesel shortly before Heschel's death. Heschel called Wiesel and asked him to come to see him. Wiesel was in the midst of a conference, but there was something in Heschel's voice that made him

---

1. Editor's note: This is not the English text as published.

leave everything and take a taxi to the seminary. "I came into his study and greeted him, but he did not speak. He cried, he fell on my shoulder. He did not say a word, he simply cried."

Bibliography

Buber, Martin. "Martin Buber." In *Philosophical Interrogations: Interrogations of Martin Buber, John Wild, Jean Wahl, Brand Blanshard, Paul Weiss, Charles Hartshorne, Paul Tillich*, edited by Sidney Rome and Beatrice Rome, 13–117. New York: Holt, Rinehart and Winston, 1964.

Dresner, Samuel H. *Heschel, Hasidism and Halakha*. New York: Fordham University Press, 2002.

———. "Introduction." In Heschel, *The Circle of the Baal Shem Tov: Studies in Hasidism*, edited by Samuel H. Dresner, v–xlv. Chicago: University of Chicago, 1985.

Friedman, Maurice S. *Abraham Joshua Heschel and Elie Wiesel: "You Are My Witnesses."* New York: Farrar, Straus, Giroux, 1987.

———. "Divine Need and Human Wonder: The Philosophy of Abraham Joshua Heschel." *Judaism* 25 (1976) 65–78.

———. "Divine Need and Human Wonder: The Philosophy of Abraham Joshua Heschel." In *Hagut Ivrit B-Amerika: Studies on Jewish Themes by Contemporary American Scholars*, edited by Menahem Zohori et al, 400–425. Tel Aviv: Brit Ivrit Olamit, Yavneh Publishing House, 1973. [Hebrew]

———. *The Hidden Human Image*. New York: Delacorte, 1974.

———, editor. *Martin Buber and the Human Sciences*. Albany: SUNY Press, 1996.

———. *Martin Buber: The Life of Dialogue*. 4th ed. London: Routledge, 2002.

———. *Martin Buber's Life and Work*. 3 vols. New York: Dutton, 1981–1983.

———. *To Deny Our Nothingness*. New York: Delacorte, 1967.

———. *Touchstones of Reality: Existentialist Trust and the Community of Peace*. New York: Dutton, 1972.

———. *The Worlds of Existentialism: A Critical Reader*. Atlantic Highlands, NJ: Humanities Press International, 1991. [1st ed., 1964]

Bibliography

Heidegger, Martin. *Introduction to Metaphysics*. Translated by Ralph Manheim. New Haven: Yale University Press, 1959.

———. "Nur noch ein Gott kann uns retten." *Der Spiegel*, 31 May 1976, 193–219. English translation: "*Der Spiegel* Interview with Martin Heidegger (1966)." Online: http://web.ics.purdue.edu/~other1/Heidegger%20Der%20Spiegel.pdf.

Heschel, Abraham Joshua. *The Circle of the Baal Shem Tov: Studies in Hasidism*. Edited by Samuel H. Dresner. Chicago: University of Chicago, 1985.

———. *The Earth Is the Lord's*. New York: Harper Torchbooks, 1966.

———. *God in Search of Man: A Philosophy of Judaism*. New York: Farrar, Straus, Cudahy, 1955.

———. *I Asked for Wonder: A Spiritual Anthology*. Edited by Samuel H. Dresner. New York: Crossroad, 1983.

———. *The Insecurity of Freedom: Essays on Human Existence*. New York: Farrar, Straus, Giroux, 1966.

———. *Israel: An Echo of Eternity*. New York: Farrar, Straus, Giroux, 1969.

———. *Kotsk: In Gerangle far Emes Dikeyt*. Tel Aviv: Hamenorah, 1973. [Yiddish]

———. *Man Is Not Alone: A Philosophy of Religion*. New York: Farrar, Straus, Giroux, 1951.

———. *Man's Quest for God: Studies in Prayer and Symbolism*. New York: Scribners, 1954.

———. *Moral Grandeur and Spiritual Audacity: Essays*. Edited by Susannah Heschel. New York: Farrar, Straus, Giroux, 1996.

———. "On Prayer." *Conservative Judaism* 25 (1970) 1–12. Reprinted in *Man's Quest for God: Studies in Prayer and Symbolism*. New York: Scribner, 1954.

———. *A Passion for Truth*. New York: Farrar, Straus, Giroux, 1973.

———. "Prayer." *The Review of Religion* 9 (1945) 153–68.

———. *Die Prophetie*. Cracow: Nakladem Polskiej Akademji Umiejetnosci, 1936.

———. *The Prophets*. New York: Harper & Row, 1962.

———. "Rabbi Pinchas of Korzec." In *The Circle of the Baal Shem Tov: Studies in Hasidism*, edited by Samuel H. Dresner, 1–43. Chicago: University of Chicago, 1985.

———. *The Sabbath: Its Meaning for Modern Man*. New York: Farrar, Straus, Giroux, 1951.

———. *Who Is Man?* Stanford: Stanford University Press, 1965.

Heschel, Sussanah, editor. *Abraham Geiger and the Jewish Jesus*. Chicago Studies in the History of Judaism. Chicago: University of Chicago Press, 1998.

————. *Abraham Joshua Heschel: Essential Writings*. Modern Spiritual Masters Series. Maryknoll, NY: Orbis, 2011.

————. *The Aryan Jesus: Christian Theologians and the Bible in Nazi Germany*. Princeton: Princeton University Press, 2008.

————, eidtor. *On Being a Jewish Feminist: A Reader*. New York: Schocken, 1983.

Kaplan, Edward K. *Holiness in Words: Abraham Joshua Heschel's Poetics of Piety*. SUNY Series in Judaica. Albany: SUNY Press, 1996.

Kaplan, Edward K., and Samuel H. Dresner. *Abraham Joshua Heschel: Prophetic Witness*. New Haven: Yale University Press, 1998.

Kohn, Hans. *Martin Buber: Sein Werk und Seine Zeit. Ein Beitrag zur Geistesgeschichte Mitteleuropas 1880–1930*. 4th ed. Eine Veröffentlichung des Leo Baeck-Institutes New York. Wiesbaden: Fourier, 1979.

Matt, Daniel C., translator and commentator. *The Zohar*. Pritzker edition. Stanford: Stanford University Press, 2004–.

Neusner, Jacob. "Remembering Heschel." *America* March 10, 1973. Online: http://www.americamagazine.org/content/article.cfm?article_id=10032.

Schneeberger, Guido, editor. *Nachlese zu Heidegger: Dokumente zu seinem Leben und Denken*. Bern: Suhr, 1962.

Silberman, Lou H. "The Philosophy of Abraham Heschel." *Jewish Heritage* 2/1 (1959) 23–26, 54.

Tannenbaum, Marc H. "Jewish-Christian Relations: Heschel and Vatican Council II." In *A Prophet for Our Time: An Anthology of the Writings of Rabbi Marc H. Tannenbaum*, edited by Judith Banki and Eugene J. Fisher, 294–314. New York: Fordham University Press, 2002.

Wiesel, Elie. *The Jews of Silence: A Personal Report on Soviet Jewry*. Translated by Neal Kozodoy. New York: Holt, Rinehart and Winston, 1966.

————. *Souls on Fire: Portraits and Legends of Hasidic Masters*. Translated by Marion Wiesel. New York: Random House, 1972.

Index of Names